W9-ADB-075

Lautréamont

The Bachelard Translations Series

Joanne H. Stroud, *Executive Editor*
Robert S. Dupree, *Translations Editor*

WATER AND DREAMS: AN ESSAY ON THE IMAGINATION OF MATTER
LAUTRÉAMONT

Lautréamont

GASTON BACHELARD

translated from the French by Robert S. Dupree

With essays by James Hillman and Robert S. Dupree

THE BACHELARD TRANSLATIONS
THE DALLAS INSTITUTE PUBLICATIONS
THE DALLAS INSTITUTE OF HUMANITIES AND CULTURE
DALLAS

Originally published in 1939
Copyright 1939. Librairie José Corti, Paris
Eighth printing, copyright 1979

© 1986 by The Pegasus Foundation, Dallas.
"Bachelard's *Lautréamont*, or Psychoanalysis without a Patient"
© 1986 by James Hillman

Cover: Drawing on paper of Gaston Bachelard by Robert Lapoujade;
collection Roger-Viollet
Design by Patricia Mora and Maribeth Lipscomb

LIBRARY OF CONGRESS CATALOGING IN PUBLICATION DATA

Bachelard, Gaston, 1884–1962.
Lautréamont.

(The Bachelard translations)
Bibliography: p.
Includes index
1. Lautréamont, comte de, 1846–1870—Criticism and
interpretation. I. Dupree, Robert S., 1940-   .
II. Hillman, James. III. Title. IV. Series: Bachelard,
Gaston, 1884–1962. Bachelard translations.
PQ2220.D723Z59 1986   841'.8   86–16866
ISBN 0-911005-08-0

The Pegasus Foundation, also known as The Dallas Institute Publications,
publishes works concerned with the imaginative, mythic, and symbolic
sources of culture. Publication efforts are centered at:
The Dallas Institute of Humanities and Culture
2719 Routh Street, Dallas, Texas 75201

Contents

Foreword

Scholars may feel that any comparison of Gaston Bachelard with that prominent figure of the sixteenth century, Erasmus, would be more hyperbole than substance. One was a man of tremendous scholarship and impressive friends, the other a self-taught student of simple tastes. But both were outstanding humanists, both concerned with the dignity and freedom of the human spirit. Erasmus possessed a mind that revolted consistently against narrowness, a description which fits Bachelard's openness as well. True, Bachelard's concerns were as widely disparate as the twentieth century is different from the sixteenth, but Bachelard's restless, wide-ranging investigations did bear a resemblance to those of Erasmus four centuries earlier. Both lived in turbulent times of extreme transition and changing values. Just as Erasmus symbolizes the rebirth of culture in his time, so Bachelard represents a new turn in the revolution of thought. He continually demonstrates how the material world impinges upon individual consciousness. To the modern student with his split sensibility, to the intellectualizing, post-Cartesian individual, he has become the prophet of a responsive, reactive, and active affinity to the world of matter and nature. Bachelard has resolved the modern dilemma of subject and object separation by proving that there can be no such dissociation.

Superficially, it may seem strange that Bachelard, occupying the chair of Philosophy of Science at the Sorbonne in the 1930s, was attracted and inspired by the bizarre figure of Isidore Ducasse, known by the pen name of "Lautréamont." Ducasse's study of animal aggression in *Maldoror* certainly seems far removed from scientific philosophy. At that time Bachelard had already established a reputation as an inventive and prodigious writer of philosophical inquiries. His eclectic thinking had carried him through journeys into little known eddies and tributaries of thought as well as into the main streams. Actually his explorations were always an odyssey, a natural, sequential voyage. He was an ever curious wanderer who had just completed his landmark study, *The Psychoanalysis of Fire* (1938) which excited French intellectual circles with his new concerns.[1] His analysis of a physical phenomenon—fire—shifted into a psychoanalysis, heralding a move from a strictly scientific study into a humanistic one. By the end of the sixth chapter of *The Psychoanalysis of Fire*, it was evident that he had fastened onto a new interest, seemingly opposed to philosophy—a study of the imagination and perception. He had begun a crucial inquiry into the constitution of consciousness, dual consciousness actually, the sense of what it means to be a subjective, sensing human in an objective, material world.

The Psychoanalysis of Fire had changed his approach from a philosophical to a phenomenological one. Here he began to use mythological themes and poetic references instead of scientific process as proof of his thesis that man perceives the world through the refracting glasses of the imagination. Henceforth, *pari passu* he would examine the source of poetic creativity. Out of this intense probing he wrote seven books leaning on poetic exposition, plus four others relating to scientific concerns. Only his death in 1962 terminated the search.

In *Lautréamont* Bachelard makes seminal discoveries in the function of the imagination as a unifying force. This is his first work, not *The Psychoanalysis of Fire*, to focus totally upon imaginative life. To say that *Lautréamont* is a study of the imagination suggests something akin to aesthetics or a study of enigmatic magic. Bachelard does not tremble at entering this field. As his analysis of the deepest human experience becomes more acute, his language simultaneously becomes that of the poet. He begins to develop his thoughts indirect-

---

1. *The Psychoanalysis of Fire*, trans. Alan C. M. Ross (Boston, 1968).

ly, like a poet. He summons images which persuade. He uses sonorous language to captivate.

It is always tempting to impute a kind of Kantian idealism to Bachelard. This book, where he reveals the more analytical side of his vision, argues evidence against that viewpoint. In probing the imaginative stance of Ducasse's sensitivity to animal aggression, Bachelard exposes the hidden complexity of human nature. He penetrates placid surfaces to expose the heart of darkness in the human psyche. Bachelard's *Lautréamont* is not intended as a crib for reading Ducasse. It is not the fascinating content of Ducasse's animal parables that intrigues Bachelard, nor any function that Ducasse's Bestiary might have as moral allegory. Instead, Bachelard delves into the nature of Ducasse's imaginative grasp of the primordial character of cruelty. Like Atlas who, Bachelard claims, is "dynamized by the mountain," Ducasse is dynamized by the aggression of animals. Bachelard the philosopher has become Bachelard the depth psychologist and literary critic.

In *Lautréamont* Bachelard reveals extensive knowledge of the work of a variety of writers. He quotes from Kafka, Kipling, Wells, De Lisle, and Whitman, along with many others. His interest in literature is not in the mere reinforcement of a particular point of view by citing a few germane lines of poetry. Bachelard initiates in this study the practice which will become more important with each succeeding concern. He invents his own variety of psychoanalysis as his means of approaching poetic works. His interest lies not in the degree to which a specific poet might be psychologically disturbed; rather he is concerned with the essential imagery which enflames the poetic imagination. He ascribes to each a unifying imaginative vortex, generally centered on one of the four classical elements.

With his sensitive eye for an image and ear for a nuance, Bachelard associates animal vitality with fire. He extends in

Lautréamont the study of the elemental images of fire initiated in *The Psychoanalysis of Fire*, especially those associated with swift, brutal, lightning change, rather than with warmth or cookery. The continuing invocation of fire imagery provides a logical link between the antipodes of Bachelard's interests— philosophy and imagination as expressed in Ducasse's animal imagery. In *The Psychoanalysis of Fire* Bachelard concluded that fire is equivalent to life. And, as he writes in *Lautréamont*: "To resist images of fire or resist those of life is the same thing."[2] Although Bachelard claims that water is his own oneiric element, he indicates that all of us need some of the spiritedness of fire if we are to be able to master the world: "One must burn with fire, break with life or continue with it" (100). His specific task, as he summarizes in *Lautréamont*, is "to show that Ducasse's images are basically active, that they are the moment of a will-to-attack, the fulfillment of a metamorphosing fieriness" (9).

Bachelard observes that Ducasse found no lag between thought and action in the savage attack: "Fieriness is a form of time, not a form of heat" (5). Time is contracted. An unexpected strike "devours time," which is "the secret of . . . insatiable violence" (1). We could turn his insight around and speculate that our twentieth-century world—accelerating, devouring time—carries an automatic price tag—the inescapable violence of the aggressive, animal energy, "those brutal impulses that are still potent in men's hearts" (3).

In addition to the fire imagery, Ducasse offers evidence of the nature of what Bachelard calls a "fertile, archaic complex" (*Psychoanalysis of Fire*, 112). Traditional psychological definition of this aspect of personality varies from his. For instance C. G. Jung defines a complex as a "splinter psyche, with an autonomous existence which, in terms of energy, possesses a value that sometimes exceeds our conscious intentions."[3] We become conscious of complexes only in our unex-

2. See below, 90. Subsequent references are in the text.
3. C. J. Jung, *Collected Works* (New York, 1953), 8:96.

pected responses, when we are especially agitated or defensive, aware of lacunae or areas of forgetfulness, when we repeat patterns, be they in our daily lives or in our dreams. In the view of depth psychologists, a complex is a psychic knot that most likely will never be loosened or only with a great deal of effort.

Generally, complexes as they push us in our daily lives are considered vexatious or embarrassing. But Bachelard extolls their virtues. He insists that poetic consistency depends upon a complex: "In point of fact a poetic work can hardly be unified except by a complex. If the complex is lacking, the work cut off from its roots no longer communicates with the unconscious" (*The Psychoanalysis of Fire*, 19). Bachelard stipulates that Ducasse's "madness"—or genius—is not random. It is unified, as is all work that is integrated in a consistent complex. Bachelard labels this complex "Lautréamontism" and demonstrates that Ducasse was more systematic and true to it than various other poets, like La Fontaine, who used less effective animal imagery.

Bachelard pinpoints the "complex of animal life," which he calls "the phenomenology of pure aggression," that he finds in the work of Ducasse. For example Bachelard draws revealing parallels between Ducasse's analysis of animal behavior and human cruelty: the claw of the crab and the human desire to clutch. Bachelard sees a similarity between an animal and the human psyche—the human is as eager to strike out as is the animal in the jungle to seize its prey. Animal cruelty slashes its victim blindly, ignores all prior relationship, invalidates previous feelings. In like manner, human cruelty returns us to the gratuitous animal gesture. Whenever we hate, the animal emerges: "In the tiniest of hatreds there is a little, live, animal filament."[4]

Unquestionably Bachelard took literary license. He strayed far beyond the few known biographical facts to construct an explanation for Ducasse's precise comprehension of the

4. *The Poetics of Space*, trans. Maria Jolas (Boston, 1969), 44.

nature of cruelty. Details never thwarted Bachelard in his search for psychic essences. His pathway led toward understanding the engagement of the will, its relationship to imagination, and the fuller utilization of each function.

The speed and energy of the animal attack is a direct lesson in the use of the projection of the will. This unrestrained, instantaneous, swift act of aggression holds, surprisingly, a secret fascination. Bachelard expresses admiration for the unleashed energy, even the joy, in the will-to-attack, "the explosive joy of the moment of decision" (10). The speed of a predatory attack breaks dull, repetitive patterns, contracts time, bypasses careful deliberation, even liberates an ecstatic excitement. It is the savage beauty of unpredictable violence in the spring of the jaguar, the hidden thrill amidst horror of Yeats's rough beast slouching toward Bethlehem. This sudden, single-minded explosion of energy is what Bachelard calls "the excess of the will-to-live that distorts beings and causes metamorphoses" (4). It is the exaltation of the pure freedom of the will.

Bachelard defines imagination primarily as the faculty which moves dynamically and metamorphoses easily. In following a bestial image through the successive stages of attack, imagination is unshackled. We can see in the mental world of slow motion, as in an old-fashioned film, each shutter-flicker, each discontinuous movement, as an animal moves toward its prey. This imaginative participation affords us a singular opportunity to avail ourselves of dynamic energy. By analogy we can visualize the intermediate stages our own cruelty takes. We should be able, in reflecting on these images, to arrest our brutal behavior by ceasing the movement of aggression before the final strike.

The breaking down of the progressive form of an act into its successive stages in order to build a new form is akin to Coleridge's definition of the process of the Secondary Imagination. Eschewing a direct or didactic approach, Bachelard demonstrates the generic avenues that lead to the subtle workings of the imaginative process. Contrary to most of those trained as philosophers, he engages his reader in the process; he doesn't just talk about it. He thereby provides direct evidence to support Coleridge's difficult formulas.

Our animal instincts, we are taught, must be held in check, must be subjugated. Again Bachelard contradicts conventional wisdom. He forces us to peer into a mirror, in which we see reflected in the animal the image of our own aggression. He demonstrates that this will-to-assail is an innate human desire which requires knowledgeable sublimation. By conversion, Lautréamontism can be transposed into an exuberance in the imaginative realm of possibilities rather than into physical action: "It is in the dream of action that the truly human joy of action resides" (90). Rather than slashing or caging our animal instincts until spirit is destroyed, he urges us to live them freely, even joyfully, but in the realm of the imagination. He warns that a "philosophy of action" too often becomes a "philosophy of agitation." He teaches us how to concentrate all the nervous, animal agitation in the imagination, husbanding it until unleashed upon constructive projects.

Bachelard argues for the retention of the spontaneity and vivaciousness of liberating animal images. These paradigmatic, bestial forms are far more than negative examples of the type of behavior to avoid. Building on the aggressive acts described so vividly by Ducasse, Bachelard attests that the freedom of spirit, the fire of creativity, can be liberated and transferred into constructive uses. Thus Lautréamontism, or the will-to-attack, provides us in Bachelard's view with the same opportunity the horse provides the rider. Like the hero Achilles or the sun god Phaëthon, we must mount and ride our steeds, celebrating the sinewy strength of their bestial nature. We can share in the joy of their animal power; we can tame their striking hooves. Through Bachelard's study of

Lautréamont, we now understand some of the excesses of the use of will and the salutary effects of the imagination.

Joanne H. Stroud
Executive Editor
The Bachelard Translations

Lautréamont

1

The Vigorous Poetry of Aggression*

> Live with such speed that you can appear to stand still.
>
> SIGNORET

> Man can bear anything, if it only lasts a second.
>
> JOHN COWPER POWYS

I

WE KNOW NOTHING about the inner life of Isidor Ducasse, who remains thoroughly concealed behind his pen name of Lautréamont. We know nothing about his personality—a book and the preface to a book are all that we really have of him. Only through his work can we imagine what his soul was like; a biography based on such insufficient data would never explain his life. The miscellaneous facts gleaned from prefaces to several editions and from various articles on his work I have postponed for a later chapter. As a matter of fact I have depended very little on such remote, indirect information in attempting this psychological commentary. On the rare occasions when a biographical detail is relevant, I shall point it out.

My objective will be twofold. First, I wish to define the astonishing unity and the overwhelming energy with which things meet in time throughout *Maldoror*. "The word," says Maxime Alexandre, "seeks action." In Lautréamont the word finds action immediately. Some poets devour or assimilate space; one might say that they always have some universe to digest. Others, far fewer in number, devour time. Lautréamont is one of the greatest devourers of time, and that, as I shall show, is the secret of his insatiable violence.

*Endnotes begin on page 93.

Second, I wish to pinpoint a *complex* that is particularly energetic. This, my second task, must be my starting point, for it is precisely the development of this complex that gives life and unity to the work as a whole and speed and giddiness to its details.

What is this complex that seems to provide Lautréamont's work with all its energy? It is the *animal life complex*, the energy of aggression. Because of it, Lautréamont's work strikes me as a genuine *phenomenology of aggression*, a pure aggression in the same sense as one speaks of "pure poetry."

The quality of time experienced in aggression is special. It is always direct yet never directed. It never swerves because of any undulation, never wavers because of any obstacle. It is a simple form of time, always continuous with its initial impulse. The kind of time peculiar to aggression is produced by a being that attacks just where existence is asserted in all its violence. An aggressive being does not wait to be given his moment but seizes it or creates it. In *Maldoror* nothing is simply passive, admitted, awaited, or pursued. Consequently, Maldoror is above suffering. He causes rather than undergoes it, for no suffering can last long when life is spent in discontinuous, hostile acts. Moreover, an awareness of the animality that subsists in our being is enough to make us feel the great number and variety of aggressive impulses there. Animal life is no empty metaphor in Ducasse's work; he presents not symbols of passions but veritable instruments of attack. La Fontaine's fables, for instance, have nothing in common with *Maldoror*. The fables are so obviously opposed to the *cantos* that a look at their differences will clarify this statement in a few lines.

In the fables of La Fontaine not a single trait of animal physiognomy is accurate, not even in the most superficial signs of animal psychology. There is no sense of animality, nothing but a transparent disguise that reveals a delight in childish doodles, little wooden circus animals, and painted pastoral scenes. Doubtless there dwells an astute psychology of human nature underneath all this pretended animal nature, yet the very psychological skill that is rightly attributed to the fabulist serves only to heighten the monotony of his animal fables. By way of contrast, Lautréamont grasps animals not as forms but as direct functions—that is, their aggressive functions. In such a case action cannot wait. Ducasse's beings do not digest—they bite. For them feeding is biting. Here the will-to-live becomes a will-to-attack that is never dormant, never satisfied, and is displayed in all its essential and frank hostility. The psychology of human society must undergo its impact to the point of seeming violated and brutally distorted, during which time the burning animal origins of our passions are revived before our own terrified eyes. To sum up, La Fontaine has written of human psychology in the form of an animal fable, but Lautréamont has written an inhuman fable by reviving those brutal impulses that are still potent in men's hearts.

From then on, all moves rapidly. Compared with Lautréamont, how slow Nietzsche seems, how calm and comfortable with his eagle and serpent. One moves like a dancer, the other springs like a tiger.

II

Positive proof of this intense animality is easy to provide: the merest survey succeeds in tracing its undeniable features. Once recognized, one finds it surprising that this animality in *Maldoror* has not been given more emphasis.

My own investigation is based on the José Corti edition, with a preface by Edmond Jaloux.[1] *Maldoror* takes up 247 pages. I have listed the various animal names that occur there and have found 185 different ones. Among these 185 the majority are repeated on several pages, often a number of times on the same page. Ignoring these repetitions, I count some

1. For the reader's convenience all of the author's references to the 1938 edition have been changed to correspond with the 1953 edition, which adds to the preface of Jaloux those of Genonceaux, Gourmont, Breton, Gracq, Caillois, Soupault, and Blanchot.

435 references to animal life. True, some are introduced by common expressions such as "stealthy as a wolf," "naked as a worm," "black as a crow." To compensate for such clichés, I have discounted about one-tenth of the references, leaving roughly 400 animalized activities.

Some pages are unbelievably dense in animals. Furthermore, this density consists of a group of impulses rather than images. Such an impulsive, willful character is therefore quite different from the roundup of ready-made animals in the works of Victor Hugo. For the poet of *Toilers of the Sea*, the animal group remains static and inert; it is merely observed. These bizarre, picturesque shapes are signs of the objective bounty of the world. For Lautréamont, as I shall show, animalized life is the sign of the bounty and fluidity of subjective impulses. It is the excess of a will-to-live that distorts beings and causes metamorphoses.

In comparison with animals, vegetation makes up at best a tenth of these appearances. It plays a merely decorative role in Ducasse's work. Flowers are often animalized: "Living camellias" draw "a human being toward the cave of Hell." When flowers are truly vegetal, they are childish: "The tulip and the anemone prattle." The sense of smell is too passive to interest Lautréamont in odors. Thus flowers appear to be improperly juxtaposed; a garland "of violets, mint, and geraniums" is an olfactory horror. Likewise, no vegetalism—the symbol of a tranquil, confident life—can be detected in Lautréamont's work. Vegetable time, continuous and curved like a palm branch, never offered its inflections to him. This absence of vegetable life makes even more obvious his polarization of life into animal speed and energy. Lautréamont's repugnance for vegetable repose is more evident if we compare his dynamic sensualism with John Cowper Powys' restful sensualism, so well described by Jean Wahl.[2]

Doubtless numbers alone will not prove a predominance of

2. Jean Wahl, "Un défenseur de la vie sensuelle: John-Cowper Powys," in *Poésie, Pensee, Perception* (Paris, 1948), 190–216.

animal life, and such a simple survey may seem ridiculous; yet I find it sufficient for an initial definition of this strange animal density, which may now be studied in more detail.

III

Now I must show that Lautréamont's is a poetry of provocation, of muscular impulse, and in no way a visual poetry of shapes and colors.

Animal forms are poorly delineated in his work. In fact they are more *produced* than reproduced. They are induced by movement, for movement creates its form as a good worker creates his tool. It would be a mistake, then, to imagine in Isidore Ducasse's life a contemplative period during which he was entertained by the thousandfold activities of living things. What one of his schoolmates tells us about his interest in natural history and an extended contemplation of the rose-beetle dormant at the heart of roses does not really point to the main axis of Lautréamontism. Animality is seized from within, in its unrectifiable, atrocious gestures sprung from pure will. Thus as soon as someone learns how to write poetry of pure violence delighting in a total freedom of will, Lautréamont will have to be reinterpreted as a precursor.

This pure violence is not human; human forms would slow down, impede, and rationalize it. When ideas, vengeance, and hatred become the explanations for violence, it loses its instantaneous, unquestionable intoxication, its shrill cry.

At that point speed loses the fundamental value that gives *Maldoror* its deep intonation, its musical certitude, its "almost impeccable artistic and literary fulfillment," as Edmond Jaloux puts it.

In my opinion this violence, instantly fulfilled in the certitude of animalized action, is the secret of active and fiery poetry. Fieriness is a form of time, not a form of heat. Before *Maldoror* revealed it, no fieriness had ever been so brutal. Jean Cassou has aptly noted the kinship between the idioms of Lautréamont and the Marquis de Sade. Nevertheless, in the Marquis de Sade the violence remains human, still concerned with an object. As Pierre Klossowski says, the result is "a lingering before the object" in Sade that would be inadmissible for Ducasse's mobility.[3]

In his *Epistle of a Werewolf*, Casanova is no better than Sade at moving beyond human limits. His "thinking uterus," only vaguely animalized, expresses nothing but a common, monotonous concupiscence. All his fieriness is human; expressed solely in metaphors, it never achieves any metamorphosis.

In Lautréamont, on the contrary, such acts are coherent and energetic enough to go beyond human limits and take possession of a new kind of soul, as I shall show.

IV

First of all, there are passages that give clear evidence of the frenzy and especially of the *bliss* of metamorphosis. "Metamorphosis never appeared to my eyes as anything other than the exalted and magnanimous repercussion of a perfect bliss that I had awaited for some time. It arrived finally on the day that I became a swine! I tested my teeth on the bark of trees; I contemplated my snout with pure delight." Then, in a subsequent passage, when the vital tension relaxes, "To return to my original shape was for me so painful that I still weep from it night after night." And in order to recover his "dazzling bulk" he will continue to wish "for the resumption, as a right, of [his] demolished metamorphosis."

Most often for Lautréamont metamorphosis is a means of executing an energetic act all at once. As a result metamorphosis is above all a metatrope, the conquest of another movement, which we might as well call a new kind of time. Since the desired vigorous movement is an act of aggression,

3. Pierre Klossowski, "Temps et agressivité," *Recherches Philosophiques* 5:104. Klossowski's study provides a valuable example of the special temporal structure of an original work.

time must be thought of as an accumulation of decisive instants in which the duration of execution matters little. The decision swells as it is asserted. The will-to-attack picks up speed, for a diminishing will-to-attack is absurd.

To understand properly this vital acceleration, one should compare Lautréamont with an author like Kafka, *who lives in moribund time.*

For the German author it seems that metamorphosis is always a misfortune, a fall, a torpor, a disfigurement. One can die from a single metamorphosis. In my opinion Kafka suffers from a *Lautréamont complex* that is negative, benighted, and black. And the proof that my investigations of *poetic velocity* and *abundant temporality* have some importance is that Kafka's metamorphosis appears candidly as a strange retardation of life and actions.

Shall I provide examples? The mother and sister of Gregor, who has been changed into a cockroach, take four hours to move a chest and never succeed. Gregor sees them through his weary eyes.[4] Then, as the metamorphosis becomes more complete, Gregor is covered little by little with a sticky substance. He clings to the walls; he lives in a coagulated world, in a viscous temporality; he hobbles haltingly.[5] He is dazed, always slow to grasp an idea, a feeling. With the least exertion he begins "to feel breathless." His whole life is an animality that wanes little by little. "He would go on slowly shaking his head for a quarter of an hour, keeping his eyes shut, and refuse to get to his feet."[6] Thus the will is broken, is dead. Gregor can take no more. If he could wish for anything, it would be the past. He lives in a time with no future.

This sluggishness is the deep, distant illness, doubtless, that brought on the metamorphosis. Gregor remembers a woman whom he wooed "earnestly but too slowly" during his adolescence, when he still had a human form.

4. Franz Kafka, "The Metamorphosis," in *Selected Short Stories.* Trans. Willa and Edwin Muir (New York, 1952), 58.
5. Kafka, 63–64.
6. Kafka, 67.

What profound diagnostic integrity Kafka's work reveals, what penetration this intimate look into progressive catatonia! If we read *The Metamorphosis* psychologically, we realize that the strange look of this work begins to recede; the author gives us a deep biological experience in which the soul's substance becomes coagulated and uncoordinated, in which movement is sluggish and disorganized, proving that there is a specific velocity below which actions become ineffective. In the general retardation of life the primary reflexes themselves end by losing their functions. Does Gregor eat? He keeps a morsel "in his mouth . . . for an hour at a time."[7] Who has not experienced in moments of weakness this organic torpor more miserable than disgust? Who has not lived through these nightmares of sluggishness and impotence, this *weariness of the organs*, this death that has lost even its drama?

In Kafka being is thus grasped in its extreme barrenness. If it is true, as Georges Matisse says, that one of the greatest calamities that can befall a living being is the inability to exercise the motor functions at any but a very reduced speed,[8] it would seem that Kafka's metamorphoses occur under a malevolent sign. Through antithesis they disclose even more thoroughly the dynamic genius that an informed reader gains from *Maldoror*.

Thus we are fortunate that Lautréamont and Kafka provide us with the two extremes of metamorphic experience. Further instances would confirm the reality and universality of such "experiences" and if we added still more, we would be able to offer a topic of great interest for analysis. This new dynamics of vitality would prove particularly useful in accounting for unusual poetic states. Then, for an appreciation of the de-animalizing power of a soul and its animalized bar-

7. Kafka, 72.
8. Georges Matisse, *La question de la finalité en Physique et en Biologie* (Paris, 1937), 2:14.

riers, it would be appropriate to construct a *bestiary* of our dreams. From this point of view, we would realize that our dreams might be appropriately placed in the realm that lies between Kafka and Lautréamont. By contemplating this bestiary which comes to life in sleep, each of us could seize upon the dynamic sense of our own metamorphoses. We would then see the transformational power of dream animals and understand how stable and monotonous, compared to their metamorphoses, are the usual categories of inanimate objects. In dreams animals are more rapidly deformed than are things; they do not develop in the same kind of time.

Perhaps at this point a personal admission can shed light on this intermediate region; I would like to define the transformism of my own reverie as a Lautréamontism in the process of being overcome. I recognize in myself a tendency to animalize my sufferings, weariness, and failures, to accept all too philosophically those little partial deaths that touch both hope and energy. But it is also with a melancholy accent, which is completely foreign to Ducassian forces, that I ring the changes on this strange and profound saying of Armand Petitjean: "Philomela dies not of love-sickness but of the lovely illness of being a swallow."[9] Man also dies from the disease of being man, of actualizing his imagination too quickly and too summarily, forgetting in the end that he could be a spirit.

Whatever may be true for these necessarily vague and fleeting intermediate forms, we must understand that they are induced, like those found in Lautréamont and Kafka, by actions and by the will. Forms are barren in Kafka because the will-to-live is exhausted; they multiply in Lautréamont because the will-to-live is incited. Let us return, therefore, to our specific task and attempt to show that Ducasse's images are basically active, that they are the moment of a will-to-attack, the fulfillment of a metamorphosing fieriness.

9. Armand Petitjean, *Imagination et réalisation* (Paris, 1936), 80.

V

Indeed, in Lautréamont metamorphosis is urgent and direct. It is executed faster than it is conceived. The subject, to his astonishment, suddenly sees that he has constructed an object. And that object is always a living being. By polarizing the vital forces, the violent desire to live fashions a particular life that is narrowly defined and a bit too specialized. In Ducasse's imagination we have the example of a summarily and therefore faultily executed creation that occurs rather too quickly, an overheated oven that "glazes" the varnish too rapidly and shapes with hostile little prickles, with sharp angles, imprisoning being in its form.

Thus we will profit fully from Ducasse's teaching if we see how nothing is to be gained from contemplating forms that are sudden and abrupt cessations. We must attempt to live out the series of forms throughout the whole of their metamorphosis and especially to live it out *quickly*.

Living at such speed gives the ineffable sensation of a litheness felt in every joint, an angular litheness opposed to Bergon's graceful evolution, that utterly spiral, utterly vegetal evolution. With Lautréamont comes a participation in the discontinuity of acts, in the explosive joy of the moment of decision. But these instants remain unpremeditated; they are savored in their isolation. They are lived out in rapid and uneven succession. The taste for metamorphosis does not go without a taste for the plurality of actions. Ducasse's poetry is an accelerating cinema from which the indispensable intermediate forms are deliberately eliminated. To follow the call of his metaphors one must go into training, and many readers abandon the poem as though they had been broken, shattered, or provoked. If Lautréamont could live with less speed, even while still living as he does, he would be welcomed into the company of the poets. . . . But did he really try? At least he did understand what it was that exhausted his reader: "Alas! I would like to develop my arguments and comparisons slowly and magnificently. . . ." But this wish is barely pronounced before poetic fire takes over his creations and multiplies them without recourse to any intermediary. Once again Lautréamont says to his reader that by going more slowly one would understand "more, if not my terror, at least my stupefaction as one summer evening while the sun seemed to sink below the horizon, I witnessed on the sea a human being swimming with great duck's feet where the extremities of his arms and legs should have been and having a dorsal fin in proportion as long and slender as a dolphin's. . . ." He has gone beyond the mere sight of a swimmer: *swimming in itself* has already come into play (the function creates the organs—feet and fin—and right along with them a horror of all that slithers along and is slimy), followed by the attack of polymorphic animality that imposes its multiple patterns of swimming, resulting in delirious, mobile *forms* that are filled with terror. The law of imagined acts makes it so, that active function of metaphor that, in a stroke of psychological genius, Lautréamont calls "an untameable and rectilinear pilgrimage."

But since it is above all movement that counts, metaphors are constantly seized at their vital roots, and we never know in which species of the animal realm desire will be realized. We never know where a gesture will discover its corresponding paw, fang, horn, or claw. It is the dynamics of exact aggression that determines the most appropriate beast. At that point, man appears as the sum of vital possibilities, as a *superanimal*. All of animality is at his disposal. Governed only by his specific aggressive functions, an animal is simply a specialized assassin. Man has the sad privilege of being able to bring it all together, to invent evil. His will-to-attack is a factor of his ambiguous evolution: "One must know that man, because of his multiple and complex nature, is not ignorant of the means of expanding still more those horizons" of his animality. Of course for Lautréamont there is no question of recovering a vanished transcendence; our horizon is vitalistic, biological. We must conquer it vitalistically, biologically. Our courageousness provides us water, air, and earth, and so we possess all realms. Man "lives in the water like the hippocamp, crosses the upper atmosphere like the osprey, and bores underground like the mole, pillbug, or sublime earthworm." This animal totality, this diversity of biological potentiality, this pluralism of the will-to-attack is "the precise criterion of a most bracing consolation."

2

Lautréamont's Bestiary

I

STRUCK BY THIS enormous biological production, this unprecedented trust in animal activities, I have undertaken a
systematic investigation of Lautréamont's Bestiary. I have
tried in particular to single out the animals he considered
most important, those he so evidently craved. A cursory
statistical survey of the 185 animals in the Ducasse Bestiary
identifies the most prominent as the dog, horse, crab, spider,
and toad. I realized quite early that these rather formal
statistics revealed very little of the Lautréamont problem and
were even in danger of misrepresenting it. As a matter of fact
this restriction of animal forms to the careful statistics of
their appearances loses what is essential about the *Ducasse
complex*: the dynamics of its vital productivity. To be accurate psychologically, then, I had to restore this dynamic
significance, the *algebraic weight* that measures the vital activities of various animals. Reliving *Maldoror* was the only
way to accomplish it. Since merely observing these living activities was insufficient, I was obliged to remain loyal to all
the intensity of Ducassian activity. And so, after adding in a
dynamic coefficient, I reworked my statistics. Naturally, I
would be pleased to know that other readers of Lautréamont
were interested in comparing my personal assessments of
these perhaps too generous dynamic coefficients with their
own responses. Still, I am almost certain that my own are ob-

jective within the broad limits traced here. They are too salient to be mere reflections of a personal impression.

The dog and the horse in *Maldoror*, for instance, are not sufficiently dynamic to be in the first ranks. They are external means. Maldoror spurs a charger or rouses a dog, but he does not get to the heart of their animal movements. Nothing in *Maldoror* can retrieve the deep experience of the centaur, an experience that is misunderstood by the ancient mythologists who see a synthesis of images rather than of acts. Thus in *Maldoror* the horse does not rear up but carries someone; the dog is limited to the aggressive behavior his bourgeois owner requires of him. His is a sort of delegated aggression; it lacks that directness peculiar to Ducasse's violence. Yet another proof that horse and dog are no more than external images, images merely observed, is that they are not *transformed*, their shapes are not inflated as are so many others in the Bestiary. The dog's muzzle does not become manifold and enact the triple violence of a Cerberus. The horse and dog have no trace of the teratological power characteristic of Ducasse's imagination. Nothing in them continues to grow or will grow forever. They stand for no monstrous stimulus at all. One concludes that animals like the dog and horse in *Maldoror* are in no way signs of a dynamic complex. They do not belong to the Count of Lautréamont's cruel coat of arms.

Furthermore, I have tried to see if the well-known declaration—"As for me, I use my genius to paint the delights of cruelty"—might not point to the main theme of his work. But there again I had to acknowledge that such anticipated cruelty, as represented by the tiger or wolf, lacked dynamic power. The orthodox cruelty implied by the image of the tiger would only hamper this complex. In any case it seems to me that these obstructed images are the ones that block the thoughts of some readers, and even as keen a critic as René Lalou cannot penetrate Lautréamontism. He finds that this beautiful phrase praising the delights of cruelty is quickly "diluted by commonplaces."[1] If one avoids beginning with the massive, readymade cruelty summed up in traditional animal imagery and tries instead to restore pluralism to cruelty, spreading it to all the functions of inventive aggression, this impression of dilution will not arise.

II

Since an overview failed to solve my problem, I have attempted to approach it another way. It occurred to me that organs of attack are the real object of study. If this is the right way to explain Ducassian aggression, that cruelty which provides the keenest delight, the animal personifying this swollen aggressive type will emerge almost automatically and everything will become clear at once. All the phases of Ducasse's phylogenesis will unfold immediately. Nevertheless, though there remains a ground for ambiguity—a most essential one, as we shall see—there will be no more confusion, no further trace of "that childishly sadistic affectation" which prejudices critical judgment.

What, then, are the means of animal aggression? Tooth, horn, tusk, claw, paw, sucker, beak, stinger, venom. . . . Almost all of these means are explicitly represented in *Maldoror*, but they are far from being equally active. For instance one cannot fail to be struck by the rarity of reptilian fauna in Ducasse's Bestiary: basilisk, boa, python and viper act only rarely. Sometimes the serpent or viper is only a sexual fantasy of the classic psychoanalytical type.[2] There is nothing surprising about this rarity, for after reflection one realizes that venomous activity is hardly suitable for a phenomenology of instant cruelty. In fact venom is a form of perfidy rather than of cruelty. Need we recall that in medieval bestiaries venom is harmful only to the veins of man (hence its name)? Nobility of blood is its own defense. A man bitten

1. René Lalou, *Histoire de la littérature contemporaine (1870 à nos jours)*. Rev. ed. (Paris, 1924), 172.
2. For the viper, cf. *Maldoror*, 123 (265).

by a reptile succumbs only inadvertently: he is caught sleeping. A strong, active man has no fear of treachery.

The horn is no more active than the venomous sting. Therefore we must not be surprised that my approach discloses only seven horned beasts among the 185 animals of Ducasse's Bestiary. The rhinoceros itself, that momentary symbol of a sluggish and inactive god with a thick hide, takes no offensive action.

The Lautréamont complex is defined in the tooth, the jaw and the beak. Something crackles and groans when the owl "in his oblique flight" bears "a rat or a frog in his beak, sweet, living food for his young." Likewise, the dogs grind up the toads with a snap of their jaws in a simple but complete and successful movement.

In such moments the mouth behind the teeth enlarges and grows cavernous; a devouring principle stretches its appetite. The mouth is enormous because the teeth are active; the poet throws himself into space as though into a mouth. Certain characteristics suggest that *Maldoror* offers a kind of *earthly food*, made up of flesh and skull and always lacking sweetness, always caught in the joy of crushing.

Yet this final characteristic is only a meagre branch of Lautréamontism. Lautréamont does not seek the meaning of life in the joy of possessing and digesting. He must find it in a more gratuitous cruelty. After eliminating the means of aggression that are weak in coefficients, we can demonstrate more clearly the fruitfulness of my approach.

III

In fact I believe that Lautréamontism is almost exclusively concerned with two themes: the claw and the sucker, which correspond to the twin attractions of flesh and blood. I have not tried to locate the fulcrum between these two factors. I believe it necessary to allow Lautréamontism this ambiguity. It is real and profound. At first the claw seems to dominate; in some ways it is faster, more obviously direct than the sucker. But the sucker provides more prolonged enjoyment. If we must choose, I would offer the sucker as the dominant symbol of Ducassian animality.

References to the claw are innumerable. It is the primary obsession of the fearful child: "Mother, see those claws. . . ." The Creator holds his prey with "the first two claws of his foot . . . as though with pincers." Conscience "can display only its steel claws." The conscience comes from the Creator: "Had she introduced herself with the modesty and humility appropriate to her station . . . I would have listened to her. I did not like her pride. I held out my hand and crushed her claws in my fingers." The struggle with the Creator is carried out claw against claw: "Yes, I see them, those green claws." He admires as a brilliant feat "a sharp blow of the claws." What pleasure he takes in contemplating the ribbons of flesh "that the claws of my master had torn from the shoulders of the young man." Finally, let us contemplate the clear symbolism of violent action from this creator of energetic poetry: "Know that in my nightmare . . . each impure animal that raises its bloody claw—that, that is my will." What, after all, would the will be without claws? To the apprentice in cruelty Maldoror says as early as the first canto: "One should let his nails grow for two weeks." The whole universe finds its claws. The Ocean itself "stretches out [its] livid claws."

The claw is therefore the symbol of pure volition. How impoverished and cumbersome is the will-to-live of Schopenhauer compared to the will-to-attack of Lautréamont! The will-to-live in Schopenhauer's theory preserves an irrationality that is fundamentally a form of passivity. It persists through mass, quantity, and totality, through the fact that the whole universe is a will-to-live. The defeat of one is automatically the victory of the other. The will-to-live is always certain to win. The will-to-attack, on the contrary, is dramatic and uncertain. It seeks drama. It is given life by the dualism of pain and pleasure. It is found in the duality of erotic and aggressive instincts. Freud, that enemy of metaphysics, did not hesitate to relate these dual instincts to the dual forces of attraction and repulsion in the inorganic world.[3] We need not go so far to realize that instinct organizes and engages in thought. It maintains thoughts, desires, and specific acts of will long enough to make these energies materialize as organs. The offensive instinct continues its movement with enough will to make the trajectory become a fiber, a nerve, or a muscle. The cruel joy of quartering spreads, sharpens, and multiplies the fingers. The relationship of the moral and the physical is therefore a formative one. The will-to-attack sharpens the point. Defense (shell or carapace) is rounded. Attack—life-threatening or sexual—is pointed. Because the will-to-attack is from the beginning a point, the thorn remains a mystery among vegetation. It is perhaps the heresy of quiet impassivity.[4]

Naturally there is no place for distinguishing clearly among claws, pincers and talons in an essentially dynamic phenomenology. All these organs seize with the same will. They truly symbolize the coming together of an organic multiplicity. Anarchy among the claws of a paw is inconceivable.

In truth Lautréamont uses "his claws" with the addition of a refined movement. Claws break more readily with a light and delicate twisting motion. There, indeed, is one of the elementary movements of Ducasse's rage: it is readily accompanied by a cruel smile. It is even difficult to imitate it without smiling: "I could take your arms and wring them like a

---

3. Sigmund Freud, *New Introductory Lectures on Psycho-Analysis and Other Works* (The Standard Edition, 22). Trans. James Strachey (London, 1964), 107.
4. A digression is no place to shed a few glimmers of light on the *mystery of the thorn* in a metaphysics of vegetalism. I am inclined to believe that utilitarian principles explain very little. Remy de Gourmont's reverie surely offers a more seductive metaphysical view. See *Le Pèlerin du Silence: Le fantôme, Le château singulier, Le livre des litanies, Théâtre muet, Pages retrouvées* (Paris, 1921), 186:

> Acacia, if your perfumed thorns are for love-play
> Gouge out my two eyes to keep me from seeing further the irony of your nails,
> And tear me with dark caresses,
> O tree with a woman's smell, tree of prey, joy of my sad heart.

In any case claws are everywhere—claws that the reverie interprets according to sexual and aggressive instincts.

wet cloth . . . or break them with a crack like two dry branches." Twisting his arms brings an adversary to his knees. Youthful violence, we should note in passing, makes use of such bullying. It leaves no trace.

The penknife, "that steel Hydra," also seems to belong to the class of sharp nails. It wounds the flesh rather than the organs. Lautréamont's cruelty never makes use of the dagger, whose effect is murderous rather than cruel.

And so, by summing up all the movements of the claw in this way and systematically replacing readymade images with functions in their attempts at synergy—in short by capturing the will-to-attack in its elementary physiology—we have arrived at the conclusion that the will to lacerate, claw, nip and squeeze nervously in the fingers is fundamental. This is the principle of juvenile cruelty. The primal consciousness of the will is a clenched fist.

IV

Now the introduction of the animal favored by Lautréamont's energetic imagination, the crab—particularly the variety called the "tourteau"—will make sense. The crab would rather lose its claw than loosen its grip. It is smaller in size than its pincers. By exaggerating the teratological tendency in Lautréamont, we could propose a crab motto: *one must live in order to nip, not nip in order to live.*

Since only biological movement is crucial for the type of imagination I am describing, unexpected substitutions are possible: the crab is a louse, the louse is a crab. "O venerable louse . . . lantern of Maldoror, whither do you guide his steps?" The fiery pages follow one after another. In the middle of the second canto appear the pages dedicated to the louse. They have been called a reckless venture into bad taste produced by a frenzy of unwholesome and puerile originality. In fact they are totally incomprehensible from the limited perspective of a static theory of imagination that allows only finished forms. But a reader who is willing to stay with this animalizing phenomenology will read with a different eye. He will recognize in it the movement of a special force, the thrust of a characteristic life. In such virulence, clearly, animality is maximalized; it thrusts forth, grows and dominates. The blood-loving louse "would be capable, through an occult power, of becoming as huge as an elephant, of crushing men like blades of wheat." Thus he must be placed in "high esteem above the animals of creation." "If you find a louse in your way, move on." "The elephant lets itself be petted but not the louse." "O louse with shrivelled eye, as long as rivers spill their slanting waters into the sea's abyss . . . as long as the mute void lacks a horizon . . . your reign over the universe will be assured, and your dynasty will extend its circle century after century. I salute you, rising sun, heavenly liberator, you, man's invisible enemy." "Filth, queen of empires, preserve in my hate's eyes the sight of the imperceptible growth of your starved progeny's muscles." The whole passage is too barbaric to be summarized. Truly it gives an impression of traveling through the "kingdom of wrath." "If the earth were covered with lice as numerous as grains of sand on the seashore, the human race would be annihilated, the prey of horrifying suffering. What a sight! I, with my angel wings, motionless in the air to gaze upon it!"

These pages have often been cited as though they were some schoolboy parody. To see them thus is to misunderstand the breadth of an original language, its dehumanized sonority pitched in the truths of an outcry. Psychologically speaking, it means refusing to live out this strange myth of metamorphoses that remains rigid and formalized in certain ancient authors such as Ovid but has been brought suddenly to life again in certain more recent ones who have returned unconsciously to primal impulses.

Despite the lessons natural history teaches or common sense would offer as wisdom, Ducasse's eagle and vulture must be grouped with the louse and the crab. The talon and the beak, which are adapted to one another in animal nature by a kind of vital synergy, must be seen in an imagination absorbed by the dynamics of animal movement as imaginatively synergetic with the claw. The eagle's beak in Lautréamont's Bestiary is nothing more than a claw; the eagle does not devour—he tears. Maldoror asks himself, "Was it my sick mind's delirium, a secret instinct independent of reason, like that of the eagle tearing at its prey, which impelled me to commit this crime?" Cruelty can have all sorts of explanations—except for need or hunger.

The eagle, like the louse and crab or all the dynamically imagined animals of the Bestiary, can change size. If combat is necessary, "he will clack his curved beak for joy." He will become "enormous." Then "the eagle is terrible and makes tremendous leaps that shake the earth." As we can see, it is always the same orgy of force—though always of a specific strength that grows in proportion to its obstacle—that must dominate resistance and bring forth victoriously the weapons of its misdeed, the animal organs of its crime.

There in a nutshell is one Ducassian line of action. So as not to tire the reader, I have omitted numerous variations of this type of aggression. Furthermore, extensive psychological investigation patterned after the dynamic rhythms of individual actions would be needed to classify the fauna of Ducasse's imagination. These dynamic rhythms are naturally more difficult to determine in less striking motions, such as those of the jackal and the rat, crocodile and cat. But such an investigation would not be useless, for Lautréamont's phantoms are marshaled by a profound nature. These phantoms are not the artificial products of fantasy; they are, in their original form, longings for specific actions. They are produced by a driving imagination of great certainty, of astonishing inflexibility.

V

Another important branch of Lautréamontism, already mentioned and quite obvious, may be rapidly examined. It is governed by the dynamic schema of the sucker. On this branch may be found the spider, the leech, the tarantula, the vampire and, above all, the octopus. The ambiguity of claw and sucker is consequently polarisable into the louse and the octopus.

Something viscous and sluggish enters Lautréamont's poetry with the spider, leech and octopus; it breaks up the monotonous domination of stark action.

Once more the swelling and multiplying of forms clearly demonstrate the energy of dynamic imagination. There is an old spider of the "larger species" that clinches the sleeper's throat with its legs; we read of the torture of its "powerful suction." "It had been a long time since the spider had opened his stomach, from which two young boys in blue gowns leapt, each holding a flaming sword in his hand. . . ." Then they speak: "an archangel, a messenger from the Lord, came down from heaven and ordered us to change into one spider and come every night to suck your throat. . . ."

Sexual pleasure, moreover, surpasses the joys of food and drink: "O octopus with your silken gaze! You whose soul is inseparable from mine; you, the most beautiful of earth's inhabitants, who command a seraglio of four hundred suckers. . . ." The phantoms of suction are always androgynous. Yet this multiplication of tentacles is surpassed in vitality and power by the creation of a new monster, the winged octopus that flies above the clouds. The dynamic imagination has been given over to a veritable frenzy of metamorphoses: "I put my four hundred suckers into his armpit and made him screech horribly. . . ." We may skip the intermediary and totally visual (hence inert) images of tentacles that the naïve imagination often compares to reptiles and listen to Maldoror continue: "[the screams] were transformed into vipers as they came out of his mouth and ran to hide in the underbrush, among ruined walls, lurking day and night. These screams, creeping along and endowed with innumerable coils, small flattened heads and treacherous eyes, have sworn to take a stand before human innocence. . . ." In the medieval bestiaries, as in Ducasse's nightmare, these images are extended by fright. The "creeping screams with treacherous eyes" last for hours: "The head of the viper severed from its body hisses for two more weeks," according to medieval "science." The hissing voice that obsesses Maldoror is the voice of his Creator. For Lautréamont the Word is violence, Genesis is Gehenna, creation is brutality.

Further, metamorphosis reverts ceaselessly to its foundations. Henceforth Maldoror is a real and monstrous octopus with eight tentacles, a knot of eight serpents; his enemy is terrified. Once again we witness this growth, this unconquerable grip: "His surprise was considerable when he saw Maldoror, transformed into an octopus, extend his eight monstrous arms toward his body. Each one, like a solid strap, could have easily circumscribed a planet. Taken off guard, he fought for a few moments against this viscous grip that became tighter and tighter. . . ."

All these images must appear artificial and repulsive for the reader dominated by a visual, panoramic or static poetics. But, for one who makes the effort to seize images of propulsion, the snake is a supple arm, even suppleness itself. The tentacle is thus the embodiment of a will that knows how to bend in order to conquer, envelop and possess. A poetics of the initial will, different from the more passive poetry of sensations, must encounter these Ducassian images.

Confronted by this longing for suction, one is naturally tempted to diagnose a form of vampirism. But in Lautréamont the symptoms are so changeable and numerous, the *states* so transitional and accordingly ill-defined, that it would be imprudent to go beyond what is given. In fact there are scenes of passive vampirism in *Maldoror* alongside the symptoms of active vampirism. Is it in this passive vampirism that Lautréamont, suffering from a superabundance of vigor, found a little calm, sleep, repose and a consoling taste of death? "I who made sleep and nightmares retreat now feel myself paralyzed throughout my whole body when [the spider of larger species] creeps up the ebony foot of my satin bed. It squeezes my throat with its legs and sucks my blood with its belly." Huysmans says that leaden slumber is one of the well-known phases of "that inadequately studied state known as vampirism."[5] Indeed, a man sleeps more soundly with a succubus than with a woman. In any case Lautréamont, the man who never sleeps, allows himself to be exhausted by the black tarantula, happy for once to lose his painful vigor. But these moments are rare, and they surprise him: "Why this tempest? Why are my fingers paralyzed?"

A more sensitive poetry, closer to human misery and as lyrical as feminine misery, would result from simply pursuing this attenuation, prolonging this too fleeting repose, and accepting this liberating defeat. Surely Lautréamont would have admired this milder echo of his pain in a poem by Jeanne Mégnen:

> I am free . . .
> and yet night rises;
> the octopus, mustard plaster of anguish,
> excavates my chest with its anxious beak,
> its eight embracing arms suck up my distress
> and make the bones of my misery crack.[6]

VI

There, perhaps too categorically, are the two great branches of Ducasse's phylogeny. Of course there are contaminations among species. Thus the octopus acquires wings, and such winged octopi seen from afar resemble crows. Inversely, in the titanic battle between the eagle and the dragon, the eagle clings to the dragon "like a leech with all its members, plunges its beak deeper and deeper . . . until his whole neck is in the dragon's stomach." His talons grip as surely as suckers. His beak stops tearing at the flesh so that it can suck blood. These interweavings of clawing and sucking actions

5. Joris-Karl Huysmans, *Là-bas* (Paris, 1891), 166.
6. Jeanne Mégnen, "O rouge, ô délivrée," VI.

show clearly, I believe, that the will for aggression keeps all its powers in readiness; Lautréamontism is mutilated when its violence is polarized in a single direction.

For the sake of completeness this very concrete study of aggressive movements must be supplemented by a more abstract one. Thus it is clear that a hierarchy of velocities explains Lautréamont's fascination for whatever swims or flies, a hierarchy that, in two instances, also governs whatever runs. We shall become aware of a complex of marine life in *Maldoror* and, loosely connected with it, a complex of aerial life.

Among fish, the dominant Ducassian creature is the shark. Lautréamont would have liked to have been "the son of a female shark, whose hunger is the friend of tempests," and a tiger. In the last pages of the second canto is an often misunderstood passage. Maldoror describes his embrace with the female shark: "In the middle of the tempest . . . in the flashes of lightning, a foamy wave their marriage bed, borne off by a cradling undersea current and rolling over one another into the depths of the abyss, they are united in a coupling that is long, hideous, and chaste! . . . At last I had found someone who resembled me. . . . Henceforth I was no longer alone in life! . . . She had the same ideas as I! . . . I was face to face with my first love." Yes, here we are confronted with love of the lower depths, a cold, icy love, which the incubi describe as the burning of the cold.

The fire of Ducasse's poetry is black and cold: "I assure you that there is no fire in my eyes, though I feel exactly as though my skull had been plunged into a helmet of burning coals. How could my innocent flesh possibly boil in a vat?" Maldoror can love only in the sea.

In the presence of such love, consciousness of evil seems so intense that it becomes the path to regaining purity. Note, in fact, the dizzying psychoanalytic *differential* in the two words brought together: "chaste" and "hideous." Pleasure could not be made more disgraceful, disgust better confirmed. One need only think about the end of the next canto to comprehend the repulsiveness of memory and the awareness of horror that *first love* impresses on certain hearts: "Royal soul, given up in a moment of forgetfulness to the crab of debauchery, the octopus of weak character, the boa constrictor of amorality and the monstrous snail of idiocy." We should note in passing that our vices are concretized in the animal kingdom. For Lautréamont, the pysche's hell is expressed in fauna.

Is consummated love a fall during a moment of forgetfulness? Must we go abruptly from Plato to Chamfort, from platonic love (the encounter of two illusions) to physical love (the encounter of two epiderms)? The epithalamium of the female shark is really a *requiem*. It intones the death of innocence, the disappointment of a pure and juvenile enthusiasm.

VII

Because of the grace and freedom of its movement, the bird symbolizes easy and joyful action in Ducasse's poems. Even so there are also singing birds in Lautréamont's work. . . .

Ducasse's volucrary is also quite varied; but apart from the eagle, which assuredly owes its importance to the relationship between claw and talon—in short, it is a flying claw—no bird is given very great value or presented as violently dynamic. The air, it seems, is a region of easy metamorphosis, metamorphosis without obstacles. When Maldoror needs to hide, all seems natural: "Thanks to a metamorphosis he mixes in with the flock of other birds without abandoning his responsibility." As it flies further into the sky, the bird becomes less individualized. It becomes a flight, even flight itself.[7] An activistic imagination has no reason to use birds other than for achieving free escape. Escape belongs to a rudimentary psychology and is therefore concretized by a schematic metamorphosis.

7. Cf. Paul Eluard, *Donner à voir* (Paris, 1939), 97: "It is not far, as the crow flies, from a cloud to a man," and André Breton, *Poisson soluble* (Paris, 1924), 89: "Birds lose their shape after their colors. They are reduced to an arachnean existence. . . ."

Again in going from fish to bird there is a contamination, and its character is quite clear when the dynamic interpretation of Lautréamontism suggested here is adopted. It concerns the simple, almost geometrical composition of flying and swimming. No one will find it surprising or odd that the *concrete* resultant of flying and swimming obtained by the essentially realistic imagination of Lautréamont is purely and simply a fishtail with wings, a synthesis of means of propulsion. Nature completes it and creates the flying fish. Ducasse's imagination creates no more than the flying tail. Nevertheless, in my view this crude puerile implementation shows that Ducasse's imagination is *natural*. The flying fish, on the contrary, is a nightmare of nature.

When the poet allows himself to schematize his creations, the power of metamorphosis is at its height. As in a nightmare, parts of different creatures come together: "He pulled the fishtail from the well and promised to attach it once again to its lost body, if it would tell the Creator that his agent was powerless to tame the angry waves of the Maldororean sea. He gave it a pair of albatross wings, and the fishtail took flight. . . ." Naturally this amputated, incongruous, stupefying genesis consisting of biological confusion has been diagnosed as madness or charged with macabre artificiality. But it simply represents a sort of vertigo of the animalizing faculty, which at this point will animalize anything. In its very inadequacy this instant biological synthesis shows clearly a *need to animalize* that is at the origins of imagination. The first function of imagination is to create animal forms.

If without searching too hastily—as classical psychoanalysis so often does—we plumb the depths of dreams, the very source of the soul's impulses, looking for human translations of dream symbols, we will be less surprised by the products of an artless imagination. Continuing an insight of the psychologist Chamaussel, Rolland de Renéville has observed that the child sometimes confuses a bird with a fish. This *confusion*—more properly, fusion—is not nonsense for a mind imbued with the permanence of forms. It is not the same for someone who takes the kinetic to be the fundamental poetic need: from swimming to flying there is an obvious mechanical homothesis. The bird and the fish live within a volume, while we live only on a surface. They have more "liberty," as mathematicians put it, than we. Since the bird and the fish have similar dynamic spaces, it is not absurd to confuse the two animal genera within the realm of impulsion and the motor imagination. If poetry truly takes on life in the beginnings of words, if it is truly simultaneous with some elementary psychic excitation, such fundamental movements as swimming, flying, walking and jumping should quicken a special poetry.

The *invitation to the voyage* is smooth and without jostling; it relies on tranquil waters. The plain and its roads extend a different invitation to the walker. The numerous distinct elements of a muscular lyricism can be readily found in the poems of a Walt Whitman.[8]

The confusion of bird and fish is also explained elsewhere. Rolland de Renéville, that sorcerer of poetic experience, correctly notes "that certain occultists assign birds and fish to a class different from those to which other animals belong. The so-called primitive painters, for their part, have left us numerous landscapes in which trees bear fish as denizens among their leaves. Above all we must not forget that this strange confusion is initiated on in the first lines of the Bible, where one reads that God created fish and birds on the same day."[9]

As though guided by a natural light and without suspecting as much, Lautréamont has thus entered into the arcana of the biological dream. He is truly a *primitive* in the poetry of energy.

VIII

This notion of the *primitive in poetry* requires long and difficult investigations that are more psychological than liter-

8. Cf. also the fine thesis of C. A. Hackett, *Le lyrisme de Rimbaud* (Paris, 1938), and by the same author, *Rimbaud l'enfant* (Paris, 1947).
9. André Rolland de Renéville, *L'expérience poétique* (Neuchâtel, 1938), 150.

ary. It would be a great mistake to seek these elements in the poetry of trouvères and troubadours. By approaching the problem along psychological lines we shall not fail to see that primitiveness in poetry—indefensible paradox—occurs late. It proceeds from the fact that in the realm of language more than elsewhere intellectual and objective (or taught) values soon become oppressive. Primitive poetry must create its own language, and it must occur contemporaneously with the creation of a language; it would be encumbered by one learned in advance. Poetic reverie itself yields rapidly to erudite reverie, even to academic reverie. To rediscover *poetic primitivism* one must get rid of books and schoolmasters.

Real courage, therefore, is needed to initiate a *projective poetry* ahead of a metrical one—just as it took a stroke of genius to discover (belatedly) a projective, truly essential geometry within the metrical one. The parallel is complete. The fundamental theorem of projective poetry is as follows: *what are the elements of a poetic form that can be distorted with impunity by metaphor while retaining poetic coherence?* Otherwise put, *what are the limits of formal causality?*

After thinking about the freedom and limits of metaphors, we see that certain poetic images are *projected* one on the other with certainty and precision, which implies that in a *projective poetry* they constitute a single, identical image. While involved in the psychoanalysis of fire, for instance, I noticed that all "images" of internal or hidden fire, buried beneath the ashes—a fire that is unseen but recovered through metaphors—are "images" of life. The projective tie at that point is so basic that one can easily translate images of life into images of fire and vice versa with the certainty of being universally understood.

The distortion of images, then, must point in a strictly mathematical manner to a *group* of metaphors. As soon as the various *groups* of metaphors in a particular poetry can be specified, we perceive that certain metaphors fail because they have been tacked on, despite the coherence of the whole group. Naturally a mind sensitive to poetry will react on its own to these mistaken additions without need of this pedantic apparatus. But it is still true that a metapoetics must undertake a classification of metaphors and sooner or later adopt the only procedure essential for classification: the identifying of groups.

More simply put, it is in the study of image distortion that we find the full extent of poetic imagination. We see that metaphors are naturally tied to metamorphoses and that in the imaginative realm the metamorphosis of being is already an adaptation to the image environment. We will be less startled to discover how prominent the myths of metamorphosis and animal fabulation are in poetry.

There are examples of projective poetry—truly primitive poetry—on almost every page of Paul Eluard's *Animals and Their Men, Men and Their Animals*. The title speaks clearly of the twin possibilities in *projection*. For a single example from the very order of images in Lautréamont that we have just examined, let us turn to the poem entitled *Fish*:

> Fish, swimmers, boats
> Transform water.
> Water is gentle and only moves
> For one who touches it.
>
> The fish moves forward
> Like a finger into a glove. . . .

A being and its surroundings cohere in this fashion: the water is transformed, it *gloves* the fish; yet the fish is also elongated, erased, enclosed. . . . This example of Eluardian correspondence, so obviously formal, would be interesting to compare with Baudelaire's powerfully material correspondences. Thus there are fresh reasons for classifying poets into two major groups according to whether they live in a vertical, intimate, internal time, like Baudelaire, or in an openly metamorphosizing one, brisk as the arrow that flies to the edge of the horizon. Such would be Lautréamont and Eluard, each, of course, translating the metamorphic life into his own style.[10] Eluard's metamorphosis is the more fluid; even his lions are aerial: "And all the lions I am depicting are alive, light and immobile."[11]

These comments are even more convincing if we contemplate the strange, reverie-inducing illustrations for Eluard's book by Valentine Hugo. Here again is an example of painting that captures the transforming power, the synchronic, dynamic painting of projective poetry. There one can indeed view a drawing inhabited by forces, matter inhabited by formal causes—the swimmer inhabited by, becoming, fulfilling the fish.

All of Eluard's other poems and Valentine Hugo's visual commentaries would support similar analyses.

In summing up these results we come to the conclusion that literary symbolism and *the* symbolism that is Freud's, such as they are executed in classical symbolism and normal dreamwork, are only mutilated examples of the symbolizing powers active in nature. Both present an expression that has been arrested too soon. They remain substitutes for a substance or person that desert evolution, syntheses named too quickly, desires uttered too soon. A new poetry and a new psychology that might describe the soul as it is being formed, language in bloom, must give up definite symbols or images learned merely and return to vital impulses and primitive poetry.

IX

Before closing this already too lengthy investigation of Lautréamont's Bestiary, I wish to draw attention to the density of his *substantialized forms*. If Lautréamont had not explored so far into *animal presence*, if he had remained happy with *function*, perhaps he might have found a less reticent audience. As I have said before, Lautréamontism could be easily

10. Cf. the chapter "Les temps superposés" in my *La Dialectique de la durée*, 2nd ed. (Paris, 1950) and my "The Poetic Moment and The Metaphysical Moment," in *The Right to Dream*, trans. J. A. Underwood (New York, 1971), 195–201.
11. Eluard, *Donner à voir*, 20.

tamed by rendering images disincarnate, toning down gestures and veiling desire. The proof resides on the level of language itself. Thus the reader would accept an adjective more readily than a substantive. He would allow remorse to be piercing or vulturelike, but for a real, red, purebred vulture—no longer mythological—to drink blood from the heart and feed on the flesh is just too much. The reader would understand a velvety, fascinating gaze or the arms of an evil temptation; but an octopus with velvety eyes, ring-encircled arms, and a mouth everywhere is false because it is revolting. All such claws have a clenched or clenching style. The veins of vermin, the furrows of fleas, the pulsing purulence—all give an unbearable impression of the alliteration of violence, of a brutality judged exaggerated because we are forced to recognize its fundamental nature.

Thus it is quite understandable that some would turn away from Lautréamont. But that is the way he is. He illustrates a complex that is clearer than all the others, a dangerous, terrifying, powerfully unnerving one. We shall see in what follows how Lautréamont's example can help to condense certain psychological observations. He represents a maximum of animalizing energy that allows us to discover energies doubtless more civilized but which still retain harsh motives, vengeful needs, and a pure will for aggression lurking beneath their subdued and moribund forms.

3

Human Violence and Culture Complexes

> Sound, arrows of honey, on the deceiv-
> ing smoky staves; tiger's eye, flashing
> hornet, velours sphinx, shuttle of misty
> song, daylight's reeds, ensteeple your-
> selves in the bee's cell, flee sharpened
> secrets, concealed in the sky, little
> feathered keys; bat, make your night-
> time overcoat in the brazier courtyards
> lined with unknown animals and
> linens. The disk is unleashed in the red-
> ness! Behold man!
>
> LÉON-PAUL FARGUE, *Spaces*

I

IN ONE SHORT chapter we may attempt to focus on this will for
power that torments yet enlivens Lautréamont, no longer as
animal instrumentality but as an intellectualized psychological principle. The result will be actions that seem more
human. Though for the weak these actions may appear crim-
inal or from a divine perspective sacrilegious, at least they
will not be so totally distorted as animal acts proved to be.
They can be grasped through the traditional psychological
categories of cruelty and rebellion. By studying them we may
return to more familiar psychological problems.

What is striking in these more strictly human acts of vengeance in Lautréamont is that they almost always supplant
struggles among equals. They attack both weaker and
stronger. Thus they are in the domain of that profound
organic ambiguity indicated earlier. They choke or claw—
choke the weak, claw the strong.

Such polarized vengeance, which will be analyzed in detail,
seems specific to *adolescent resentment*, for it is especially dur-

ing adolescence that the ambivalent complex of active resentment is shaped. Then vengeance against the weak and
against the strong takes different forms. A companion is
brutalized; a teacher is made fun of. Finally in adolescence
school rivalries provide numerous delights whose crudeness
and exhibitionism are thinly veiled. To be first is a great
Ducassian privilege: you get to show your rear end to the
others. In the winter sky the crane leading the triangle "has
the privilege of displaying its pinfeathers to cranes of inferior
understanding."

It is amazing that no one has been tempted to do a psychology of bullying and rivalry. An entire book would be needed
to clarify it, focus on its individual and social characteristics,
and pinpoint the reasons for its persisting and for the indif-
ference or impotence of teachers toward this monstrosity
that stamps both bully and bullied with its dual ill-fated
marks. Bullying is more serious in the school environment
than elsewhere because it occurs at the same time as educational training. My thesis in this chapter suggests once more
that the adolescent learning period was painful and intellec-
tually irritating for Isidore Ducasse. In a general way a psychoanalysis more intellectualized than in its classical form
would be improved by a closer look at educational conditions. A psychoanalysis of learning would rapidly identify
specific complexes at their sedimentary level—*cultural complexes* above the lower levels of Freudian psychoanalysis that
are the result of premature fossilization.

From a purely social point of view the slight difference in
age among adolescents is exaggerated by distinctions in grade
levels, so that a rhetorician can easily impose his will to
specific power, in its intellectual form, on his eleventh-grade
colleagues. Furthermore, this facile vanity is put to an abrupt
test by the "superiority complex" of the teacher. He who was
formerly triumphant is now wounded by a thousand arrows
—arrows of honey!—in the sarcasm of his teacher. From

vanity triumphant to vanity crushed there is only a few hours' interval. This double emotion running through the school hours has been poorly gauged. People suppose too readily that vanity is automatically corrected by ridicule. In reality even in those forms of rivalry that seem harmless, vanity occasions very painful repression. As a result adolescence is deeply disturbed in the learning effort by the impulsions of vanity. Plagiarisms, penalties, unarguable matters of taste, cutting criticism without objective proof—these are the aftermath of the rhetoric class. Elsewhere, in the *Preface to a Future Book*, there is an apology for plagiarism as a healthy literary exercise: "Plagiarism is necessary. Progress implies it. It moves in close to an author's sentences, uses his expressions, cuts out a false idea and replaces it with the right one."

However, the psychological problem of literary training still remains to be examined in its strictly linguistic features. In fact the rhetoric class is, in the mathematical sense, a recursion point for the evolution of the expressive life. It is there that language should be reshaped, straightened out and corrected under the Olympian mockery of the master. There it truly becomes doubled by conscious etymology. For the first time the mother tongue becomes the object of strange suspicions. For the first time language is supervised.

Every poet, even the most direct, has passed through a period of language reflected on or meditated. If he makes use of an ineffable etymology, if he suddenly gains the grace of naiveté, he becomes so conscious of it that he returns to it as a ruse. Anyone who has reflected on language in solitude while listening to countless books without the schoolroom reflections of the *corrector*—a man elevated by two podium steps—is truly too happy. There are no poetic souls without manifold, prolonged echoes, echoes on echoes, without an essential multihumanism, a word heard in plains and woods, in the infinite and in the hermitage, in light and shadow, tenderness and anger.

II

These brief remarks, seemingly far from my topic, will nevertheless clarify certain problems in Lautréamontism. They
take into account the often childish qualities of its impreca-
tions, the academic imitations that recall Musset, Goethe,
Byron and Dante throughout *Maldoror*. They also serve as
commentary on certain information that contemporaries
have revealed concerning Lautréamont's school life, the
times when the fiery poet suffered the mockery and even the
punishment of a rhetoric teacher hostile to free imagination.[1]

Only an evocation of unhappy schooltime can help us
understand the passage in which Lautréamont, swallowing
his own tears, drinks "long sips from that cup, trembling like
the teeth of the pupil who looks out of the corner of his eyes
at a man born to oppress him. . . ." How could an arbitrary
education in which the teacher feeds "with confidence on the
blood and tears of adolescents" fail to leave an inexpiable
spite in the heart of a young man? "When a boarding student
in school is governed for years that seem centuries, from
morning to evening and evening to dawn, by a pariah from
civilization whose eyes are constantly on him, he feels the
tumultuous waves of a living hatred rise like a thick smoke
into his brain, which feels as though it were ready to burst.
From the moment that he has been thrown into this prison
until the final one of his departure, an intense fever jaundices
his face, pulls his eyebrows together, and hollows out his
eyes. He meditates at night because he does not wish to sleep.
During the day his thoughts leap over the walls of his brutal
environment until he escapes from it or is thrown out, like a
plague victim, from this eternal cloister. . . ."

When reading *Maldoror* one cannot fail to be struck by the
number of references to the dignity of hair. At a time when
Sarcey's letter on beards destroyed the career of a holder of a

1. Cf. François Alicot, *Mercure de France* (January 1, 1928), 199–206.

degree, what must have been the severity of the school cen-
sor who enforced the official propriety of hairstyle on pupils?
During schooltime did not Isidore Ducasse suffer from "inability to express oneself in a hairstyle"? "Do I not remember
how I myself was scalped, even though only for five years (the
exact period of time escapes me)?" Five years is, more or less,
exactly the time that Ducasse was locked up in the prisons of
a Pyrenees university. From then on if one considers seriously that the least disturbance can have a very great impact on
an adolescent, one would acknowledge without hesitation a
scalp complex that is a metaphorical form of *castration complex*.
This scalp complex, with all its sexual components, is readily
apparent in *Maldoror*: "Who, then, has scalped you?"
"Perhaps you have no forehead." They promise that the hair
will grow back, since "animal hair, when it is cut, grows back
longer," but can adolescents with shaved heads really recover
pride in their virility? This is the origin of the nightmare that
ends the fourth canto: "Take away, take away that hairless
head, polished like a tortoise shell."

III

But let us see more precisely how Ducasse's violence, still
marked by culture complexes, is polarized in its humanized
form against the child and against God. The child in his
physical weakness and the young comrade in his intellectual
backwardness are constant temptations for violence. But
with Lautréamont, for whom all is individualized, it is the
son of the family of man that he wishes to ravish, the well-
protected son, so different from the Montevidean child,
already exiled at the age of fourteen without hope of return.
Violence against this anxiously protected son is intellectualized, becomes self-conscious. While animal violence is executed without delay, in frank criminality, violence against
the child becomes savage in its hypocrisy. Lautréamont
makes falsehood an integral part of violence. The lie is the

sign of man *par excellence*. As H. G. Wells puts it, "An animal may be ferocious and cunning enough, but it takes a real man to tell a lie."

Thus every passage in which a crime against a child occurs has a dual duration. Time is divided into acting and meditating components, and these two kinds of time do not share the same interweaving or linking principles, the same causality. When planning a crime against a child in very great technical detail, Lautréamont gives an impression of *suspended time*, so that in certain pages—absolutely basic, though all too few—he is able to give the temporal essence of menace, of deferred aggression. As soon as Lautréamont threatens, he no longer slumbers. This absence of sleep is at one with the absence of laughter. The jasper eyes are in synergy with the bronze lips. Eye and mouth await in concert.

Then too, Lautréamont tires quickly of threats. The son is not really guarded well enough; the cage of the family is too poorly defended. After rejoining decent, reasonable men, Lautréamont has the impression of entering into the company of beavers. Was he familiar with the legend from the *Book of Treasures?* "The beaver or portico dog is hunted for his sexual organs, which are very useful in medicine. The beaver is aware of it and bites them off while being chased so that he can be left alone."[2] He is castrated by persuasion.

Likewise the child or the good pupil. The child is a wonderful detector of power. Training has produced in him some exquisitely conditioned reflexes: a child—especially a good child —cries when given a stern look. Any unskilled apprentice in violence, even a teacher utterly lacking in vital energy, can easily monitor his progress in the art of threatening by watching the reflection of *anguish* in a child's or timid pupil's face. In the end, as an encouraging mark of success, the child gives back good for evil, tenderness for cruelty: "You will do

2. Charles Victor Langlois, *La connaissance de la nature et du monde au moyen âge, d'après quelques écrits français à l'usage des laïcs* (Paris, 1911), 382.

evil to a human being and you will be loved by the same being: that is the greatest conceivable happiness."

Remaining faithful to the psychoanalysis of schooling that
has been our inspiration, let us transfer these observations
concerning childhood to adolescence, and we shall again discover love or respect for the teacher, a replica of the castration complex in metaphorical guise. In fact to the child with
his "tender flesh" and "soft bosom" there corresponds the
adolescent, with his unsophisticated vocabulary and his uncertain syntax, whose throat tightens at the slightest claim
that he has committed a solecism. However, adolescents
could easily deflate the obviously exaggerated rage of the
teacher of "good taste" and "pure language" by ridiculing
him. Yet they let the teacher retain—as the requisite symbol
of this mutilating education—the shears of his stylistic cri-
tiques.

IV

The child is only a pretext for the apprentice in cruelty or,
more precisely, for the transition from physical to moral
cruelty. Maldoror dreams of a greater enemy, of the most
conscious enemy of all. The result is a challenge to the
Creator, a challenge at once brilliant and sensual. Concerning this point I can be brief, since the fine book of Léon
Pierre-Quint has already brought this aspect of Lautréamontism to light. In particular Pierre-Quint has identified the
juvenile Cainism in the work.[3] I shall confine myself to
underscoring adolescent resonances, so palpable in the work
of a young poet.

In his pride as instructor, the teacher sets himself up every
day as the intellectual father of the adolescent. An obedience
that in the realm of education ought to be a pure awareness
of truth then begins to taste unbearably of irrationalism

3. Léon Pierre-Quint, *Le comte de Lautréamont et Dieu* (Marseille, 1929). Cf. 97 in
particular.

because of this paternalistic usurpation. It is irrational to obey a law before being convinced that it is reasonable. Likewise, is not man the child of his Creator? Are not various unrelated virtues required of him, is not an a priori method of moral life imposed on him? Now all these virtues and methods—like the rhetorical devices we have been discussing—are systems of obedience. They link actions in so swift a fate that we forget the ineffable moments of impulse, the first instant of taking a breath. Then the virtuous life becomes altogether monotonous, a naked piece of obedience, just as literary life is too academic, too closely modeled after schoolboy heroes, too cold a piece of eloquence. Real life and language must come from revolt, from conjugated, eloquent revolt. One must *pronounce* revolt, speak it to the schoolmasters, to *the* Master: "Well," cries Lautréamont, "I introduce myself as a defender of man, I who hold all virtues in contempt."

The creatured creature will, through violence, become a creator. Thus in a literary system, precise reactions to the acts of creation are deliberate rather than merely passive metamorphoses. Metamorphosing reactions are violent because *creation is a form of violence.* Suffering already experienced cannot be eradicated except through projected suffering. The sorrows of giving birth are compensated for by the cruelty of conception. Consciousness fed by remorse and the past—by an ancestor personalized in the father or schoolmaster or God—is inverted, according to Lautréamont's teaching, and becomes certainty of power, will for a future, the sure light of a *person* intoxicated with plans. Everywhere and for everyone, along every line of progress, we discover this fatal compensation, this law that equates arbitrary action and violent reaction, the law of the equality of revolt and creation. Even more precisely, violence and revolt appear to certain minds as the only consequence of a *personal* destiny. Disobedience, for someone untouched by either grace or reason, is an immediate and decisive proof of autonomy. Whoever creates *persons*, must he not also expect revolt? The immediate function of a person is to revolt. A person requires a special inspiration to find restraints and not be irritated by obstacles, a special courage to reject the impulse toward explosive rebellion. Lautréamont has done nothing to moderate this initial revolt; he pushes it immediately to its extreme. When is rebellion the most intense? From all evidence, when directed against the strongest adversary. Thus we can come to understand the truly dynamic equilibrium that is the reciprocal incitement between Creator and creature: "He fears me, I him." Generally speaking, a mythology of power must create simultaneously both violent and revolting gods.

V

Thus the lines of this axis reveal a Lautréamontism raised almost inevitably to a blasphemous pitch. But here we must emphasize that this life-driven inflation is the result of literary expression. In short, Isidore Ducasse's life was peaceful. Nothing in it recalls the actual revolt carried out by a Rimbaud, nothing of the fiery mobility of "the man with the wind for soles." At this point, as I have said before, it seems unnecessary to look beyond his *school career* for an explanation of Isidore Ducasse's writings. It is a drama about schooling, born in a writing class, a drama which must be resolved in a work of literature. Doubtless we should not slight the sufferings. But it is no less true that the real rebel does not write or, at least, stops writing when he rebels. Without scorning revolt Jean Paulhan rightly remains on his guard against "anyone who arrives by a linguistic and quasi mechanical route."[4] Just so, written revolt is the exact reaction to what Paulhan calls "rhetorical Terror," a sort of

4. Jean Paulhan, "Les Fleurs de Tarbes," *Nouvelle Revue Française*, 46 (1936), 856–69.

Cerberus that is the violent guardian of a closed etymology, a linguistic Hades in which words are only the breath of shades, poetry a deformed and bruised remembrance.

It seems to me that my interpretation of Lautréamontism as a group of *cultural complexes* also fits perfectly with the conclusion of a fine article by Ramón Gómez de la Serna: "Among the punishments that are imposed [on Lautréamont] for eternity is having to copy over endlessly the conclusion of his third canto. 'Count, you will copy for me an eternal number of times the end of chapter three,' God must have told him with the austerity of a schoolmaster who commands that the verb 'to have' be copied a hundred times. What a frightening punishment! And Lautréamont has written and rewritten since then the conclusion of the third canto; and he gives his useless copies to the Creator, and the Creator rips them up and awaits more to follow." During this time, "the very ones who have failed God, not his sons nor his grandsons but those from the beginning of the world, nip at the Count of Lautréamont."[5] The classroom is hell and hell is a classroom.

As we can see, the schoolroom atmosphere surrounding *Maldoror* has not escaped Ramón Gómez de la Serna. Nor has it escaped André Malraux. *Maldoror* is the echo of a drama of education. One should not be surprised that learned literary critics, who too often are themselves teachers, remain untouched by it.

5. Ramón Gómez de la Serna, "Image de Lautréamont," in *Le cas Lautréamont* (Paris and Brussels, 1925).

4

The Biographical Problem

I

THE DETAILED STUDY of Ducassean frenzy that I have worked out in its two forms—animal and social—will perhaps allow us to inquire about the problem of Lautréamont's "madness" in a somewhat clearer fashion. An examination of this problem will show how much progress psychiatry has made in the course of the last century. Psychiatry has studied the enormous field of aberrations, vesanias and transitory accidents that leave a penumbra around the clearest of minds. Conversely it has disclosed in the most disturbed of souls certain syntheses that are yet coherent enough ways of thinking for leading one's life and creating a work of art.

How strikingly hasty are the peremptory judgments of certain literary critics. Speaking of the Lautréamont case, a psychologist as acute as Remy de Gourmont does not hesitate or doubt that it is madness.[1] He simply makes it the madness of a genius, thus agreeing with conventional psychological opinion. He finds that throughout *Maldoror* "consciousness is on the wane," though a simple reading shows, on the contrary, an astonishing crescendo, the inflexible line of a perfectly homogeneous spiritual destiny that is never unfaithful to its first impulses. Nor is his judgment of the *Poems* any better. They reveal, he says, "the state of mind of a dying man who repeats, in the midst of a distorting fever, his most distant memories—that is, for this child the teachings of his

---

1. Remy de Gourmont, *Le livre des masques: portraits symbolistes, gloses et documents sur les écrivains d'hier et d'aujourd'hui.* 12th ed. (Paris, 1921), 139.

instructors." Gourmont speaks again of a work that develops, "ferocious, demoniac, disordered, or exasperated with
pride in demented visions. It bewilders more than seduces."
As though one must always seduce! Lautréamont does not
care to seduce; he wants to carry away his prey in a single
stroke. He is insidious only in order to upset the reader's
systematically sluggish, non-dynamized imagination. Once
again Ducasse's poetry must not be analyzed in terms of
visual images but of kinetic ones. The poetry must be judged
as a system especially abundant in reflexes, not as a collection
of impressions. A good preparation for this examination
would be to consider the work of Paul Schilder and Henry
Head on patterns of posture, which are also thoroughly
studied by Jean Lhermitte in his *The Image of Our Body*.
Upon returning to *Maldoror* after reading these modern
works, one notices that Ducasse's writings contain innumerable *bodily images*, accelerated active projections,
gestures with no viscosity at all. All these activities are the
evidence of a life of pantomime that cannot be recounted
without recourse to special biographical principles. By
reading *Maldoror actively* and evoking our muscular sympathies within, we comprehend what a hygiene of pure will
might be. When we have experienced relief in an exclusively
internal physical training that aims for purity of impulsion,
we succeed in composing a kind of *central gymnastics* that gets
rid of the worry of executing muscular movements, yet leaves
us the joy of determining them. In my conclusion I shall
develop this theory more extensively, thus instituting a Lautréamontism that is more candidly virtual in character. I
mention this now simply to show how Gourmont errs in presenting Isidore Ducasse as a restless person. Ducasse is not
restless but active; he is an activator.

Léon Bloy is no better a psychiatrist than Remy de Gourmont: "The author," he says, "died in a padded cell, and that
is all we know about him."[2] There is no point in drawing at-

2. Léon Bloy, *Belluaires et Porchers*, 1884–1894 (Paris, 1905), 5.

tention to the inaccuracy of the statement. Literary judgment can also seem contradictory: "As for literary form, there is none. It is liquid lava. It is crazy, black, devouring." But further on, in a sort of unacknowledged but invincible sympathy, Bloy realizes that Lautréamont bears "the indisputable mark of a great poet . . . a prophetic unconsciousness." This is a profound judgment that contradicts, point for point, the opinion of René Lalou who, we may recall, disclosed in Lautréamont "a thirst for originality." Recognizing prophetic power does not prevent Bloy from concluding: "It is an alienated man who speaks, the most agonizing of alienated men."

Bloy also thinks that he has found signs of autoscopy in Lautréamont, but here again one must distinguish. Where did he see Lautréamont appeal to "his sick liver, his lungs, his extravasated bile, his sorry feet, his clammy hands, his polluted phallus, and the hair standing up on his head out of fear"? In fact when organic awareness is specified in Lautréamont, it is always the awareness of a power. The organ is not described there as disturbed, pain-ridden or lazy, like a kind of fragmented madness that would produce obsession, phobia or fear and benumb psychological life. It seems rather that Lautréamont's endoscopy is always a pretext for the production of a self-confident energy. This endoscopy enlightens the consciousness of the most dynamized muscle. Then, like the string of a living lyre, there resounds an element of muscular lyricism. The harmony is filled in by itself; a specific muscular awareness draws the whole body along through synergy. An active epicureanism reflecting general pleasure in various organs by requiring an awareness of healthiness in every function would be physically dynamogenic. It would develop an anatomical pride rarely expressed but nevertheless constituent of a *natural history* for unconscious thought. Lautréamont has produced such a precise, detailed, analytical dynamogeny. There is no enlightened self-indulgence without this clear and distinct homage to particular organs.

The white wine from my region is tasted with the kidneys. Again, Ducasse's active endoscopy has nothing to do with the morose physiology depicted by Léon Bloy and so frequently evidenced by the writings of Huysmans, who in this context is the antithesis of Lautréamont.

More recent authors use this word "madness" just as carelessly without taking account of the complex relationship between consciousness and unconsciousness. Thus they are led to psychological contradictions. So René Dumesnil would place Lautréamont—not, it is true, without some misgivings —among fantasy writers "because of his strange life itself and his exceedingly fantastic writings, where madness sometimes takes the place of genius. Lautréamont is indeed a fantasy writer."[3]

We can see that literary critics have no notion of the complexity of madness. An even stranger ignorance is evident in the way that they fail to penetrate the significance of a notion indispensable for understanding the basic psychological function of literature—that is, the notion of *madness written down*. Literary criticism has failed to pursue, through all their detours, these strange minds that have the rare ability to write down their complexes in an explicit fashion. A complex is essentially unconscious, and as soon as it rises to the center of language, it is liable to exorcism. When it is embodied in written language, a further problem arises. And finally it is not simply up to the moment of publication that the author's psychic state changes. Certainly the word "sublimation" is misused in current psychoanalytic criticism—with particular impropriety when applied to turns of thought linked in uniform causality that follow, without developing, what I have described elsewhere as the axis of "vertical time."[4] But in the process of literary creation sublimation takes on a more definite meaning. It becomes a true objective crystalization. Man is crystalized in the peculiar system of the book.

3. René Dumesnil, *Le réalisme* (Paris, 1936), 202.
4. Bachelard, "Poetic Instant and Metaphysical Instant."

Never has a progressive crystalization been so clear, perhaps, as in Lautréamont's case. Two sorts of evidence may be presented.

First, we must pay tribute to the verbal assuredness of the work, to its resonant coherence. Without the help of rhyme, without the guardrail of strict meter, sounds are linked as though driven by a natural force. Edmond Jaloux is right, in speaking of this acoustical assuredness, to recall the lessons taught by Flaubert. At bottom there is the same homogeneity. Never has a violent piece of writing been less scattered. In its very aberration it is not aberrant. It is a madness lacking in insanity, a system of violent energy that fractures the real in order to live out its *achievement* without scruple or embarrassment. Lautréamont personifies a kind of *fulfillment principle* that makes the *reality principle*, rendered ponderous by its passivity, pale by comparison.

Second, after this very positive proof of intellectual liberty, we can observe equally clear evidence of liberation. In fact a complete change of attitude has never been so total as the one separating Lautréamont from *Maldoror*. Once the first canto was printed, it appears that Lautréamont became a stranger to it, indifferent or perhaps even hostile to his own work. "You know," he says in a letter, "I have renounced my past. I now sing only of hope. . . . [I] have, at the same time, corrected six of the worst pieces in my damned book." If Lautréamont had lived, he would have created poems in a completely different way. And one cannot help recalling Rimbaud's silence as a comparison with the sudden criticism that emerges in the *Preface to a Future Book*. In both cases they have completely changed their minds.

Furthermore, even from the point of view of the basic Ducasse complex it appears that the sixth canto already shows evidence of this effacement. Twenty pages before the end, the animal imagery is reduced almost to nothing: no new animals appear in the Bestiary. The tone thus becomes less brilliant, and an ear attuned to the preceding cantos already senses that the last notes are near, that the complex has just about unwound the last loop of its skein. Poetically and psychologically *Maldoror* is thus a completed work. It constitutes a season of genius. In the *Preface to a Future Book* several animals recur, most often in bundles, like worlds of living images reshaped by the unconscious. With the slightest polemical impulse the poet resumes his "scorpion-tail whip." But he knows that from now on metamorphoses have passions as their seeds. To describe the passions, "one need only be born somewhat of a jackal, a vulture, a panther." He will thus be silent about his passions. "If you are unhappy . . . keep it to yourself."

If we had of Dostoevsky only *Notes from the Underground*, we might diagnose him as being equally pessimistic. But as soon as the mind can vary its language, it becomes the master. Now concerning Lautréamont we have certain evidence of this diversity. Lautréamont dominated his own phantasms.

I must add, finally, that the ability to maintain impulsion in a verbal form and the total absence in his life of any wild activities alone suffice to prove Lautréamont's mastery of his complexes. Nothing in his life is *strange*. He comes from Montevideo. He moves to France to study in a lycée. He goes to Paris to do mathematics. He writes a poem. He has trouble getting it published. He prepares another work that more prudently takes into account the publishers' timidity. He dies. There is not an incident and especially not a single action that reveals anything *strange*. One must therefore return to the work itself, enter it completely—for it has an inspired insanity—and then the test of originality can begin.

No, originality truly cannot be willed. Other thinkers during the time Lautréamont was writing doubtless strained to be original, yet the majority of them joined some school or other. It is to the point that only three poets in the second half of the nineteenth century founded schools without knowing it: Baudelaire, Lautréamont and Rimbaud. They are masters who were acknowledged later, after their deaths, who imparted nothing, who provided no commentary and never explained themselves. To shed any light on their lives and resolve the biographical problem we must return to a contemplation of their work.

This is likewise the conclusion of Gil Robin's fine article, which appeared in a special issue of *Disque vert*. Robin has caught in its organic origins the "verbal sprout" that impelled Lautréamont to write. The word is not determined simply by external sensations or expressions of perception related to the five senses: "The kinesthesia of tangled voices possesses a cruel and precise language for Lautréamont." At no time, Robin notes, does one feel the intellectual fatigue, the verbal fatigue or slight echolalia that recalls favorite terms and familiar assonances in certain styles. For then verbal melody lacks profundity. On the contrary Lautréamont is "sonorous and symphonic in the manner of Berlioz." Finally, Robin develops an argument that seems to me very convincing and instructive. If it were a question of some mental alienation, "the work would be *incommunicable* to a normal mind. It is a fundamental quality of alienation that he who suffers from it becomes strange to us in the original sense of the word. Now since Lautréamont's death, there have been numerous poets who have been attuned to *Maldoror*, who have loved and been inspired by it." I cannot insist too much on this point, for I believe that Lautréamont's is a very coherent work that draws its cohesion from the oneiric and poetic activities of numerous generations. At the beginning of the era of relativity, Painlevé says of the fifty mathematicians gathered around Einstein, "Look, you can *see them understanding*," in order to demonstrate the soundness of the new theories to those who can't understand them. The same must be said to those who rage about the liberties taken by surrealists: "Look, you can *see* them understand Lautréamont." As soon as they are felt in their instantaneous and conjoined impulsions, Lautréamont's actions bring us, in Braille, news of our innermost night.

Despite his reservations Dr. Jean Vinchon arrives at the same conclusions. If we speak of alienation, that is because Lautréamont stood apart from the psychology of his time. He is both a precursor of the psychology of the abyss—of which psychoanalysis is an example—and the postural psychology of Head and Schilder. Lautréamont, Dr. Vinchon tells us, "appealed to all the obscure forces of the unconscious that swarmed within him, like the beasts of his own *Maldoror.* . . . From worry and anxiety, he followed the emotions through tears, grimaces, exasperation, failures and lies. He penetrated willingly into the realm of spleen and irritability. He skirted every anomaly while seeking the secrets of mystery. But he came to himself after having pushed his explorations further than anyone before him."[5]

Returning from these explorations one feels strange in the ordinary world. As André Breton has rightly noted, Ducasse's imagination "makes you aware of so many other worlds at once that soon you don't know how to behave in this one."[6] However, one might add, a reader devoted to reading Ducasse's writings understands that ordinary experience in ordinary life is—like all unified experience—a monomania. To live a life that is simply human and pursue a predetermined social career is always to be the victim, more or less, of an obsession.

II

We shall have another example of the artificial nature of external biography when we look at the problem of Lautréamont's mathematic abilities. All the biographers refer to his talent. What proof do they offer? Only this: Lautréamont crossed the ocean to take examinations at the Ecole Polytech-

5. Jean Vinchon, "La folie d'Isidore Ducasse . . . ," in *Le cas Lautréamont.*
6. André Breton, *Les Pas Perdus* (Paris, 1924), 200.

nique and at the Ecole des Mines. At least that is what was claimed when no one knew about his long sojourn at Tarbes and at Pau.

Is this really enough? Must all candidates for the Ecole Polytechnique be said to have mathematical talent? The Ecole Polytechnique is to mathematics what a dictionary of rhymes is to Baudelaire's poetry.

What the biographer does not say the work sings out. Several pages in Lautréamont are quiet and elevated; these pages are a hymn to mathematics: "O severe mathematics, I have not forgotten you since your erudite lessons, sweeter than honey, filtered into my heart like a refreshing wave." These four pages could be given a detailed commentary, but they would not shed the light of certainty on the problem of his talent. Nevertheless a mysterious note has suddenly been struck, a certain seriousness has appeared in the work, and if we are not certain of having found in Lautréamont a mathematical mentality, we have at least the impression of probing a mathematical soul. It seems that the fiery poet had a sudden nostalgia for discipline, that he recalled the times when his impulses were arrested, when life was overcome in him and he could think, when he loved abstraction as a lovely solitude.[7] For us this is extremely important evidence of a soul under *supervision*. Mathematics cannot be done without this supervision, this constant psychoanalysis of objective knowledge that frees the soul not only from its own dreams but from its ordinary thoughts, its contingent experiences, which curtails its clear ideas and seeks in the axiom its automatically inviolable rule.

These four mathematical pages appear in *Maldoror* right after the most excessive passages. Lautréamont has just presented his exaltation of the louse and crushed the "lump of animated matter" made up of interwoven lice that he will throw upon mankind like bombs of hideous life, these packets of vermin. And at this point Reason appears with a

7. Ducasse, *Poésies II*, in *Oeuvres complètes* (Paris, 1953), 383.

strange gentleness: "During my childhood you appeared to me one May night in moonlight above a green meadow on the banks of a clear brook, and all three were equal in grace and modesty, all three majestic as queens." It is for the sake of arithmetic, algebra and geometry that Lautréamont writes of "this night in May." There we can feel the soft, poetic extension of a heart in some fashion non-Euclidean, intoxicated with non-love, joyous in refusing the joy of living abstractly in a non-life, of moving beyond the obligations of desire, of breaking up the parallelism of will and happiness: O mathematics, "he who knows and appreciates you no longer wants the goods of the earth; he is content with your magical delights." Thus at one stroke the reader has been transported to the antipodes of the life of action and sensations.

Perhaps I should also point out a note barely perceptible in this passage, one that must always be reawakened when mathematical training is recalled. It is precisely violence, a cold and rational violence. There is no mathematical learning without a certain spitefulness of Reason. Is there a more fixed, swift, icy irony than that of the mathematics teacher? Squatting in the corner of the classroom like a spider in his crevice, he waits. Who has not known that horrid silence, those deadly hours, the exquisite retardation of torture in which the best of students suddenly loses, along with his self-confidence, the dynamics of his locked-up thoughts? A loss of speed breaks his forward momentum. Is there not some distant memory of intellectual maltreatment in this imprecation of Ducasse: O mathematics, "he who has not known you is a madman who deserves to undergo the most terrible tortures, for there is a blind contempt in such an ignorant lack of concern"?

To foist reason on someone seems to me to be a noteworthy kind of violence, since reason is compelling enough in itself. And I cannot free myself from the notion that creeps into my mind under so many forms that *harshness is a psy-*

chosis, the particular professional psychosis of the teacher. It is more serious for the mathematics teacher than for any other, for harshness in mathematics possesses coherence. Its necessity can be demonstrated; it is the psychological aspect of a theorem. Only the mathematics teacher can be both severe and fair at the same time. If a teacher of rhetoric—having lost the benefit of his discipline's lovely, mild relativity—is severe, he is partial too. At the same time he becomes a robot of a teacher. It is, therefore, easy to avoid his harshness, for it can never succeed. An energetic student has a thousand means for weakening or deflecting his teacher's harshness.

I scarcely need add that in the realm of adolescent education, as in child rearing, harshness causes neurosis. It is no surprise that the mathematical mind itself can be so painfully scarred by the school years. At the time of its special training the mathematical mind can have multiple, delicate, contradictory tastes. The mathematical mind is as diverse as the poetic mind, but they bear the onus of harshness, mockery and cold demonstration in different ways. It may be that *Maldoror* is a reaction to the ill humor of a teacher in the Pyrenees. At any rate we may be tempted to find some personal action of some teacher to account for this profound phrase of Lautréamont: "The theorem mocks its own nature." Yes, there really are mocking theorems; others are hypocritical and perverse, others boring. . . .

Viewing the drama of Ducasse's thought, Léon Bloy imagines just this sort of conflict between the elements of rational training: "The unknown catastrophe that made this man mad must . . . have struck him at the very heart of the exact preoccupations of science, and his wild anger against God must necessarily have been a mathematical anger."[8] In fact there seem to be the traces of two different conceptions of the Almighty in Ducasse. There is the Almighty who is the creator of life. It is against this creator of life that

8. Bloy, *Belluaires et Porchers*, 16.

Ducasse's violence revolts. There is the Almighty who is the creator of thought. Lautréamont places him in the same cult as he places geometry. "The Almighty revealed himself completely, in all his attributes, in that memorable labor which consisted of bringing your treasure of theorems and your magnificent splendors out of the bowels of chaos." In the presence of these productions of mathematical thought contemplated in "supernatural meditations," Lautréamont genuflects "and his veneration pays homage to [their] divine visage, as to the proper image of the Almighty."

As we can see, an adoration of thought is part and parcel of an execration of life in Ducasse. But why did God make life when he could have made thought directly? This is the drama in Ducasse whose depths Léon Bloy has seen perhaps better than anyone else. In any case it is striking that in the middle of *Maldoror* poetry modifies its rhythm at the same time as blasphemy fades and this clearing of silence and light is in the very heart of a sort of virgin forest, full of monsters and cries and given over completely to the double frenzy of murder and birth.

In another canto, a single phrase recalls mathematics; it speaks of the beauty of the pursuit curve. This tiny fact allows us to suppose that Lautréamont went beyond his preparation for the Ecole Polytechnique, that he was not just a simple student in a special mathematics class who was poorly equipped, as we know, for the monotonous study of conics. It would seem then, from this slight indication, that Lautréamont led a life of somewhat freer scientific studies separate from the rhythm of assignments and advanced beyond the level of university competitive exams.

To sum up: personal mathematical training, a poetry sure of itself, a language with precise sonorities, a power of poetic induction tested by the extensive authority of the work, is this not a set of proofs that guarantees us the integrity of his mind?

III

We can now see that contemplating a profound work leads us to ask psychological questions which a detailed biographical examination could never answer. There are minds for which *expression* is more than life, other than life. "The poet," Paul Eluard says, "always thinks about *something else*"[9] Applying this point to Sade and Lautréamont he goes on to say, "For the expression 'You are what you are,' they have added, 'You can be something else.'" In general what can a biography offer to explain an original work, an obviously *isolated* work, a work in which the literary workmanship is lively, brisk and blockaded, from which daily life, as a result, is expelled? Finally, one reaches those works that are negatives of positive life. No developer will reverse their shades. They must be accepted in their attempt to break up. They must be understood within their own system as non-Euclidean geometry is understood within its own axiomatics.

Just so, *Maldoror* can be taken as a pretext for understanding what a work would be if it were somehow to tear away from ordinary existence and welcome that other life which must be designated by a contradictory neologism as an *unlivable life*. Here in fact is a work born not from the observation of others but not exactly from the observation of oneself either. Before being observed it was created. It has no goal yet is an action. It has no plan yet is coherent. Its language is not the expression of a previous thought. It is the expression of a psychic force that has suddenly become a language. In short it is instant language.

When surrealism rediscovers Lautréamont's traces, it will enjoy the same catachreses; it will break up familiar images even if it must bring together "a sewing-machine and an umbrella on a dissecting table." The essential thing will be to center the word in the aggressive instant by freeing oneself

9. Eluard, *Donner à voir*, 73–84.

from the sluggishness of a procession of syllables appealing to the musician's ear. In effect one must move from the realm of images to the realm of actions. The poetry of wrath is thus opposed to the poetry of seduction. The sentence must become a schema for angry mobiles, set in motion by a series of psychic explosives, not by parceling out "explosives" through pedantic phonetics. It suffices to say that the explosion is not syllabic but semantic. It is the meaning that explodes, not the breath. The *fracturing word* of Lautréamont and the good surrealists is therefore created less to be *heard* in its outbursts than to be *desired* in its sudden decisions, in its joy of deciding. Its energetic meaning cannot be grasped through diction; one must accept an active, vigorous induction and feel its induced virility. Thus Vladimir Mayakovsky sang:

> A cry twists my mouth to a crumpled curve.
> Then:
> like a jittery bed-ridden patient
> up jumped
> a nerve.[10]

A stimulated state of soul and not a comforted one is the prequisite of Ducasse's teaching. Doubtless there could be innumerable investigations in that direction. They would extend the experiences of poetic psychology. But poetry is more readily passive; it returns to mystery as to the fold, to instincts as to forces, to life as to destiny. It loves to pursue a story, tell a tale of life, turn love into fiction. In other words poetry has an almost invincible tendency to return to life, to enter within life, to live out gently the continuous time of life. We should not be surprised that the example of Lautréamont remains isolated and that in putting aside the fundamental habits of life he eludes the very principles of biographical study.

10. Vladimir Mayakovsky, "A Cloud in Trousers," in *Mayakovsky*, trans. and ed. Herbert Marshall (New York, 1965), 101.

IV

However, since some readers may perhaps not have in mind the few dates that mark the life of the poet, let me sum up quickly what I have learned from the various studies I have read.

Various biographers differ, even while announcing their slender hope of linking Lautréamont's writings with his times, on the date of the poet's birth. For René Dumesnil, Lautréamont was born on April 4, 1850. The day and the month are right but the year wrong. Other writers indicate 1847. In fact Isidore Ducasse was born in Montevideo on April 4, 1846.[11] Remy de Gourmont says that the poet died "at the age of twenty-eight."[12] This error is repeated by several critics. Actually, Lautréamont died at twenty-four, on November 24, 1870. The certificate of death was signed by the manager and valet of the hotel where he died (rue du Faubourg-Montmartre, no. 7, Paris).

Concerning his ancestors we now have some exact information that corrects old errors. This information seems to come from the book on Lautréamont and Laforgue by Gervasio and Alvaro Guilloz Munoz published in Montevideo.[13] The father of Isidore Ducasse, François Ducasse, was born near Tarbes in 1809, and his mother was also born in France, in 1821. François Ducasse was a teacher in Sarguignet, a small community near Tarbes. His signature is to be found on public registry documents in 1837, 1838, and 1839. In 1840 François Ducasse emigrated to Uruguay.

The question of what happened to François Ducasse and his fortune is of no great interest for this specific investiga-

11. Ducasse, *Oeuvres complètes*, 405.
12. *Ibid*, 17 and Gourmont, *Le Livre des Masques*, 139.
13. Guillot-Munoz, Alvaro & Gervasio, *Lautréamont et Laforgue* (Montevideo, 1925). I was unable to obtain this work. It was described in a review by Valéry Larbaud, "Lautréamont et Laforgue," *Nouvelle Revue Française* 26:114–16.

tion. Some say he died wealthy, others poor, long after his son's death. In 1860, when his only son was sixteen, François Ducasse sent him to France, where the young Isidore began his secondary-school studies. François Alicot has found evidence of a period at the Tarbes lycée, then at the Pau lycée. I have used Alicot's article (published in *Mercure de France*) several times. One should refer to it for information about Lautréamont's school years, at least as they appeared to some of his colleagues.

In the special issue of *Disque vert* (Paris, Brussels, 1925) there is a good Ducasse bibliography edited by Raoul Simonson. The first canto of *Maldoror* appeared anonymously in August 1868. There is general agreement that the work was written in 1867. The G.L.M. edition provides, along with other information, variant readings where there are differences between the 1868 and 1869 editions of the first canto.

Some of Lautréamont's Paris lodgings have been identified. He is known to have rented a piano. Through an effort of sympathetic imagination Philippe Soupault has reconstructed Lautréamont's Parisian period with plausibility, despite erroneous information from the biography available to him at the time of writing. But once again the facts are too scanty to throw any light on Ducasse's psychology. We must always return to the work in order to understand the poet. A work of genius is the antithesis of life.

5

Lautréamont: Poet of Muscles and Cries

I

NOTHING IS MORE inimitable than fundamental or primal poetry, nor is anything more primary. It commands a life, commands life itself. By communicating it creates, for the poet must create his reader and not merely express common notions. A prosody must impose an interpretation and not simply regulate phonemes, effusions and expressions. That is why a philosopher who looks for the working of metaphysical principles in poems recognizes without hesitation the *formal cause* within poetic creation. Only the poetic cause, which mingles beauty and form, can give beings the vigor of seduction. There we see no facile pancalism. The beautiful is not a simple arrangement; it needs power, energy, conquest. Statues themselves have muscles. The formal cause is of an energizing order. So it is at its peak in life, in human life, the life of the will. A form cannot be properly understood through idle contemplation. The contemplating being must play out his own destiny before the universe he contemplates, and so all types of poetry are types of destiny. A history of poetry is a history of human feelings. For example an attentive psychologist will gauge the fine book by Marcel Raymond, *From Baudelaire to Surrealism*,[1] as a veritable *summa* of new psychological discoveries. He will doubtless be struck by a single fact: almost all these new discoveries concern the will. In its astonishing variety contemporary poetry proves that man desires a becoming; he desires it for his very heart. Raymond's book provides us with multiple avenues to

1. Marcel Raymond, *From Baudelaire to Surrealism*. Trans. G. M. (New York, 1949).

an inventive affectivity, a normative affectivity that renews and orders all the powers of being.

From now on the beautiful can no longer be simply *reproduced*. First of all it must be *produced*. It borrows from life—from matter itself—elementary energies that are first *transformed*, then *transfigured*. Certain poems belong to transformation, others to transfiguration. But always a human being must undergo a metamorphosis by means of a true poem. The principal function of poetry is to transform us. It is the human creation that transforms us most rapidly; a single poem can do it.

Unfortunately all too often heteronomous images destroy the law of active imagery. An implausible mimeticism parodies a movement that is health-giving or creative only in its innermost recesses. Thus when schools dominate and aesthetics is taught, the metamorphosing powers are arrested. Only a few solitary poets are allowed to live in a state of permanent metamorphosis. For loyal readers they are models of tangible metamorphosis. Certain direct poets bring about a sort of induction, a rhythm of the nerves in our feelings that is different from linguistic rhythm. They must be read as examples of vigorous life, as examples of an original will-to-live. And so I have attempted to relive the inductive force that runs throughout *Maldoror*. I have devoted lengthy months of docile and sympathetic experience to the study of this poem in attempting to recover the specific ferment of a life quite different from ours. In this chapter I would like to show, without offering a complete film of its images, how poetic dynamism is brought into play in Lautréamont and pinpoint the principle of his *active universe*.

II

At the threshold of Ducassean phenomenology I would propose placing the following theorem of dynamic psychology so well articulated by F. Roels: "There is nothing in the understanding that was not first in the muscles." This is an accurate paraphrase of the old device of the sensationalist philosophers who found nothing in the understanding that had not first been in the sensorium. In fact a large part of Ducasse's poetry emerges from the myopsyche described by Storch. The reader who is submissively sympathetic with *Maldoror* can feel this myopsyche reviving within him almost fiber by fiber. An animalized imagery helps him reach that curious state of muscular analysis. It seems in fact that animal life makes a coefficient of specific muscles and organs to such an extent that the whole animal is often the servant of a single organ.

With Lautréamont the consciousness of having a body does not remain a vague awareness, a consciousness slumbering in a happy warmth. On the contrary it is elucidated violently in the certainty of having a muscle, is projected into an animal gesture men have long since forgotten.

The gentle Charles-Louis Philippe gazing at a child in his cradle says: "His feet move about nicely, looking a bit crazy, and you might think that each toe is a separate little mechanism." Most often it is in time of fatigue, when muscles are relaxing, that we have an impression of such animalized gestures. Yet Lautréamont discovers his power in the most active hours, in those gestures that most take the offensive. His true liberty is his consciousness of muscular choices.

III

An example of the direct, initial character of quivering muscularity appears immediately in the first pages of *Maldoror*. Hate with its "proud, wide and lean nostrils" suffices to restore muscular primitiveness to a worn, deprived being, exhausted by its most passive sensations. Then the quivering of nostrils no longer replies to the invasion of perfume; the pride of a nostril dynamized by hatred is fed by no incense. "Your nostrils, which will be immeasurably dilated by ineffable contentment, by immobile ecstasy, can ask nothing better of space, as it were having become embalmed by perfumes and incense; for they will be sated by complete happiness."

Is there any clearer example of the reversal of perceptual qualities? What had been passive sensation has suddenly become willed. What had been expectation has suddenly become provocation. Is not smell the most passive, most earthly and immobilizing of the senses, the one that must slowly, patiently and knowingly wait for the reality forced upon it to move away, to fade so that it may truly dream of it and write its poem? When the aroma is a memory, the memory will be an aroma. Perfume with its matter and its ideal can be integrated into richness and vast correspondences. But what is gained in richness is lost in decision. A primitive dynamogeny like the one that enlivens *Maldoror* cannot allow triumphant aromas. All this passively breathed universe weakens and fades when action asserts itself as a universe. The one breath conquers all others. Life on the offensive overtakes life offended. At that moment living flesh becomes an aroma unto itself.

IV

Thus the smallest muscle that opens a nostril or hardens a look incites a special life and poetry. In his *Etudes philosophiques sur l'expression littéraire* Claude Estève has given the proper place to this variety of muscular syntax: "There is no sensation that does not sound an alarm for all the muscles. All the means of action and reaction quiver together at its call." With Lautréamont the world does not need to invite us to act. Maldoror approaches reality with poetry in his wrists, massages and kneads it, transforming and animalizing it. If only matter were flesh to be murdered! "Fury, with its curt metacarpus," forces its form onto a brutalized world.

We would be mistaken, however, if we thought of Ducasse's violence as a disorderly one that is intoxicated by its own excess. Lautréamont is not a simple precursor of "paroxysm." Even during his energetic tempests the muscular sense keeps its freedom of decision. As Henri Wallon has shown, the boisterous child has real centers of boisterousness. Lautréamont, the boisterous poet, does not allow confused violence. He does not allow diffused reactions or confused actions. He designs actions. He knows how to administer his aggression. Doubtless he must have had to suffer from classroom immobility like so many of us. He underwent the postures of the seated adolescent, the schoolboy limited to the articulate pleasures of elbow and knee, going his way and flapping his elbows—what an image of sly humanity! Under the teacher's eyes Isidore Ducasse twitched his head hypocritically, exaggerating the tic in his neck to hide the primitive impulse with a slow, drawn out movement. "Like a condemned man who tries out his muscles while thinking about their end when he is soon to mount the scaffold, standing on my straw bed with my eyes closed I twist my neck slowly from right to left, from left to right for hours on end." To understand such passages in dynamic fashion one must eliminate the visual image—in this instance the scaffold. Then one can give proper attention to the obscure back neck muscles which are so near the head yet so far from consciousness. By dynamizing these muscles, one discovers quite simply the muscular principles of human pride, so little removed from the lion's. The psychology of the neck and its technique are extensively taught in *Maldoror*. By contemplating these lessons we can better understand the importance of ruffs, collars and ties for a psychology of majesty.

If such an explication could be developed at greater length, we would realize that physiognomy has almost completely forgotten the temporal aspects of the face in describing the anatomy. These aspects are revealed when the dynamics of gesture are brought to life again in a total syntax by distinguishing various phases of energy, particularly by establishing the proper hierarchy of the nervous system in its manifold expressions. The face of a man who has made up his mind manifests the instants of mutation in his existence. Common sense is so poor an observer that it lumps all his expressions under the single rubric of an *energetic face*. Lautréamont is not thus frozen in his energy. He ceaselessly protects his freedom, mobility and determination.

V

We shall find new evidence of the primitiveness of Ducasse's poetry in the prominence given to *cries*. Those who desert this perspective on the primeval as a hierarchy of energies find cries to be only accidents, fragments or archaic survivals. On the contrary energetic primitiveness demonstrates that cries are not rallying calls or even reflexes. They are essentially direct. A cry does not call—it exults.

The cry is also the antithesis of language. All those who have dreamed while watching a solitary child have been surprised by his linguistic play: the child plays with murmurs, babblings, liquid voices, the tones of fine little bells that ring without resounding—delicate crystals that a breath would break. The linguistic play stops when the cry returns in its initial strength, with its gratuitous anger clear as a sonorous and energetic *cogito*: I cry out, therefore I am an energy.

Once more the cry is in the throat before being in the ear. It imitates nothing. It is personal; it is the person who is cried. If it is reined in, it will ring out in good time, like a revolt. You torture me, I am silent. I will cry out only on my day of vengeance. Then await a black cry in the night. My offensive is a sombre sword. My vengeance stands out in sharp relief against the darkness. It signifies nothing, yet it is marked with all my being. Those who utter piercing screams do not know how to cry out. They have put the cry behind their fear instead of in its primeval place before all threats.

Every intermediary between cry and decision, every word, every secret must be silenced. "Now it has been over for a long time; for a long time I have spoken no word to anyone.

O you, whoever you are, when you are next to me, may your vocal cords allow no tone to escape . . . or you yourself attempt in any way to make me understand your soul by the use of language."

Isidor Ducasse's statement has not, perhaps, been given sufficient emphasis: "They say that I was born in the arms of deafness." The psychology of the person born deaf who is suddenly capable of hearing has never been worked out, though the psychology of such a man, born blind and then cured by Cheselden, has been reimagined endlessly. If Isidore Ducasse was born deaf, it would be interesting to know at what age he could have heard with astonishment that "I myself am speaking. Using my own tongue to emit my thoughts, I realize that my lips move. . . ." Then he would be listened to up to the very limits of hallucination when he hears the twilight unfold its gray satin sails. . . .

But in reading *Maldoror* and giving it a sort of sonority of the nerves, that is by adding sounds to pure impulses, we would see that weak voices are those that have been weakened. We must return to the cry and recognize that the first word is a provocation. A *howl* gives birth to Ducasse's phantoms or at least puts his stumbling phantoms back on their feet.

To understand this energetic hierarchy, we must return again and again to the almighty power of the cry, to the moments when the screaming being thinks that his cry is guaranteed "to arrive at the farthest reaches of space." Such a fundamental cry denies physical laws as original sin denies moral ones. Such a cry is direct and murderous. It bears its hatred into the very heart of its enemy like an arrow. "It seemed to me that my hate and my words, leaping over distances, annihilated the physical laws of sound and arrived distinctly in their ears, muffled by the bellowing of the wrathful ocean." Thus human cries contribute to an angry universe. The "forthright mouth" has discovered its vowel.

VI

How could such a cry establish its syntax? Despite all active anacoluthons, how can a rebellious being lead to action? That is the problem solved by *Maldoror*. Everything in the body is articulated when the cry, itself inarticulate but marvelously simple and unique, speaks the victory of power. All animals, even those least on the offensive, articulate their war cry. But all forces are parodied in Nature. And in the manifold animal life that Lautréamont lived out he heard warlike cries that were "droll chuckles." He heard cries that are born from within the biological mass. It is this same thought that Paul Valéry utters through Monsieur Teste: "The gentle were bleating, the bitter were caterwauling, the fat were bellowing, the thin were screaming." One must move up to the human to attain dominating cries. In the midst of this poetic fracas we can hear them make their way through the cantos of *Maldoror*. Those who see in these cantos a theatrical curse are mistaken. It is a special universe, an active one that is cried out. In that universe energy is an aesthetic.

6

The Lautréamont Complex

> We entered the drawing room to rest.
> M. Lenoy walked in front of us; sud-
> denly he stopped and stepped back for-
> biddingly. We went forward.... An
> enormous panther, crouching in the
> back of the apartment, stared at us
> with his shining, ferocious eyes. His tail
> was raised around his spotted sides and
> his jaw partly open, giving a view of
> long white teeth that did not reassure
> us. This animal was so artfully stuffed
> that it was impossible not to believe it
> alive.
>
> *Letter of Leconte de Lisle,*
> cited by Estève

> Leconte de Lisle heard howling on the
> beach of the Cape two wild dogs whose
> sorrowful barking he would interpret
> only years later. He saw baboons and
> ostriches. He even had the chance to
> look at two lions up close—alive this
> time—a male and a female. Of course
> they were in a cage. "The male is only
> two years old and already magnificent;
> his leaps are frightening and sublime.
> When he roars, the walls of his prison
> shake." But more than fierce animals,
> stuffed or not, he was interested in the
> ladies of the country....
>
> Estève, *Leconte de Lisle*

I

To assess properly the importance of a complex and understand the multiple meanings of a psychology of complexes, it
is often interesting to see an improperly grafted complex in
action, a complex riddled by contradictions, held back by
scruples. Sometimes the complex also conceals some of its
character by the mere fact of being artificially sublimated,

adopted without faith like a means of expression considered complicated but nevertheless comprehensible to everyone. In each case, insufficiency or avoidance, the dynamism of the complex is falsified; but this error, this arrest, suddenly allows us to understand a psychological mechanism that remains secret so long as it functions normally.

I am going to examine different instances of masked or sclerosed *Lautréamont complex*. In their attenuated forms, lessened in energy, these examples will seem repugnant or ridiculous. I will be accused perhaps of forcing works that from another angle still appear beautiful and alive into a deforming pigeonhole or a pedantic system of analysis. That is always the reproach leveled at those who try to compare different casts of mind, for such a comparison always ends more or less by denying them any real originality. It is clearly more attractive to go right to the essence of the individual, to affirm his integrity, and to share with perfect sympathy the profound inner world and originality of the intellectual hero under examination. But just here a paradox arises: *Originality is by necessity a complex, and a complex is never very original.* It is only by meditating on this paradox that we can recognize genius as a *natural label*, as a nature being expressed. If originality is powerful, the complex is energetic, imperious, dominating. It leads the man; he produces the work. If originality is slight, the complex is masked, false and hesitant. In any case originality cannot be analyzed completely on an intellectual level. Only the complex can give a dynamic index of its originality.

Literary criticism, then, would gain from a deeper study of the psychology of complexes. It would be led to reexamine the problems of influence and imitation. To do so it would have to substitute *transference* in the psychological sense for reading. Sympathy is too vague a form of communion; it does not change the souls it brings together. In fact we can only understand ourselves clearly through a sort of psychic induction by exciting or synchronically moderating our impulses. I can understand another soul only by transforming my own, "as one transforms his hand by placing it in another's."[1] A genuine communion is necessarily temporary. It is discursive. In the life of the passions—our usual life—we can only understand ourselves by *activating* the same complexes. In a philosophic life, smiling and serene or disappointed and painful, we can understand ourselves only by *reducing* the same complexes all together, by diminishing all tension, by abjuring life.

If this double meaning of variation is not taken into account, it is because of a failure to grasp the essentially dynamic nature of a psychology of complexes. A complex can only be understood through a course of activation and reduction.

II

Let us begin by examining the case of an artificial Lautréamont complex—that is, a poorly formed one.

A very obvious instance is displayed with all the complacency of its strategy throughout H. G. Wells's *The Island of Dr. Moreau.* Its curiously impoverished premise is familiar: By slashing muscles and viscera, resecting bones and dislocating joints, a surgeon constructs "men" from animals, part by part, out of animal stuff. The scalpel is handled like a pencil; to change a being around it is enough to adjust its shape. To modify the features of the whole, one need only move a characteristic organ around. Grafting a rat's tail on its nose creates a miniature elephant. That is the way a child works when he draws. This English novelist works the same way when he "imagines."

A shipwreck victim arrives at just the right moment on the island of surgical mysteries to personify fear and disgust in the face of such an enterprise. A spectator is given the affective reactions, thus gratuitously relieving the surgeon of them. Such an *analytic* method, which divides up the ele-

1. Eluard, *Donner à voir*, 45.

ments of the complex among several characters, forestalls any psychological plausibility. A complex must maintain its synthesis of opposites; it is in the sum of gathered contradictions that the strength of the complex is measured. For a Lautréamont complex, however stifled certain harmonics might be, it is necessary to retain a primeval ambiguity of fear and cruelty. Like lava and ashes, fear and cruelty emerge from the same crater.

Naturally, to get us back to reality—another way of supposing it hasn't been left behind—Wells imagines that brute nature has been imperfectly subjugated by Dr. Moreau's craft. The deaf forces of race limit the power of this attempt at constructive biology. The odor of blood, the sight of carnage liberate these imperfectly channeled dynamisms, and the novel ends with the rebellion and revenge of the animals, who prove that their inner destinies are invincible.

This entire artificial biology is supposed to be sustained by a few rudimentary scientific observations; this effort at rationalization, an obvious pretense at the beginning of the novel, ends suddenly. Wells himself senses it; his positivist spirit is suddenly touched by a nostalgia for mystery. To make his fiction plausible and conceal its simplistic character, its look of grim masquerade, he presents a narrator at the end of the novel who is halfway between reason and madness, reality and dreams. So in its last pages the novel perhaps gains some psychological interest, since there we enter the truly formative kernel of the story.

This formative kernel is, in my opinion, a Lautréamont complex but one lacking vigor, developed with little accuracy or sincerity, and incapable of producing a powerful work yet nevertheless sufficient for the author to go on with his bogus and boring fiction.

What is Ducassian about this kernel? It is as lacking in energy as it could be; it does not point to an active force, an irresistible temptation, utterly visual in appeal. It is the strange habit of *seeing* a particular animal in a human face.

This was the leading idea of Lavater's physiognomy, which was markedly successful at the end of the eighteenth and during the first half of the nineteenth centuries. This habit is a kind of sympathy with the power of expression and the need to express. It hinges on a clue and stabilizes a fleeting attitude, placing labels on faces with the alacrity of a Creator. It imposes forever the names of animals on a man or family. It even gives the werewolf legal status. Messrs. Leloup, Lelievre, Lechat, Lecoq, Lapie, Lerat, Lecerf, Labiche, Leboeuf are the names of faces from times past. And vice versa when a writer gives a character the name of an animal, he unconsciously gives him the matching face. Referring to a gunner in his *Stello*, Vigny comments quite naturally on "the long head of my peaceful Badger."

We find a certain satisfaction in looking at a human face thus animalized. Are we pleased by our dominion over an animal thus recognized? Are we proud to stand as man before an inferior brother that bears the indelible mark of animality? At any rate once we have classified a face according to Lavater's principles, we have the naive impression that the main part of psychology has been achieved. We anoint ourselves physiognomists and, *therefore*, as psychologists. We enjoy our discovery with a laugh. Sometimes however we feel the encroachment of a certain disquiet concerning this reduction of the human visage. We fear animal action and revenge, assuming that such a violent face already implies real violence. It is evident that there are reasons for a simplistic affectivity. The narrator of Wells's novel seems to have been haunted by the various possibilities of an animalization that would link Lavater's characteristics to Ducasse's slumbering energies. Thus Wells puts us onto the traces of a psychological relationship between Lavater and Lautréamont: "I can witness that for several years now, a restless fear has dwelt in my mind, such a restless fear as a half-tamed lion cub may feel. My trouble took the strangest form. I could not persuade myself that the men and women I met were not also another, still passably human, Beast People, animals half-wrought into the outward image of human souls; and that they would presently begin to revert, to show first this bestial mark and then that." "Then I look about me at my fellow men. And I go in fear. I see faces keen and bright, others dull or dangerous, others unsteady, insincere; none that have the calm authority of a reasonable soul. I feel as though the animal was surging up through them. . . ." "When I lived in London . . . I could not get away from men . . . and prowling women would mew after me, furtive craving men glance jealously at me, weary pale workers go coughing by me, with tired eyes and eager paces like wounded deer dripping blood. . . . And even it seemed that I, too, was not a reasonable creature, but only an animal tormented with some strange disorder in its brain, that sent it to wander alone, like a sheep stricken with the gid."[2]

Let us consider the rather large number of adjectives in this passage and do the opposite of what I suggested in a preceding chapter as a means of attenuating Lautréamontism. Let us place a specific animal behind a harsh face, a fleeing animal behind a furtive act, a mewing animal behind feminine lamentations, another with a powerfully hungry mouth —in short, let us restore the missing Lautréamontism to these passages. Then we shall see them in their true colors and understand their proper complexual synthesis.

In any case we have found the sore spot in a work presented within an unconvincing rational mechanism, and it is here that the complex has been "scientifically" sublimated so facilely in *The Island of Dr. Moreau.* The author presents the complex, this slight neurosis, as a consequence of the spectacle he has sketched; he presents suffering as the result of a painful memory. But even a psychologist only somewhat aware of the psychology of complexes could not be deceived: the germ of the book is to be found in its closing pages. A

2. Herbert George Wells, *The Island of Dr. Moreau,* in *Seven Famous Novels* (Garden City, N. Y., 1934), 155–56.

psychoanalyst will always take this last confession to be the original element of the drama.

Such a psychoanalysis could be applied to *The Jungle Book*. But the more subtle and profound psychology of Rudyard Kipling would not reveal so clear a design. That is why I wished to use Wells's work as a first example of the way this theme can be used to illustrate a completely *depoeticized* schema that satisfies a mediocre need for plausibility by masquerading as scientific explanation and is made frivolous by the attempt to be entertaining. As a result almost all the functions of a literary work are forgotten.

III

I shall attempt to follow the development of a Lautréamont complex in a more poeticizing fashion, even though Ducasse's language is not recoverable in all its power. Indeed, some of Leconte de Lisle's poetry gains a special psychological sense when read psychoanalytically as a Lautréamont complex— poorly executed doubtless and yielding more cries than actions but still explaining a very great number of images.

First of all there is de Lisle's bestiary. It is not so rich as Ducasse's; certainly it does not have a real phylogenetic power. It has no ability to translate desires into metamorphoses. Animals always appear in it as complete and fully mature. They appear in a naive, facile brutality, in a cruelty that cannot be subtly elaborated as are Ducasse's phylogeneses, but which comes to a sudden halt in a traditional form, pondered in its picturesque features. It is not difficult to show that the synergy of actions is poorly described, that it has not been experienced in its living complexity. Lautréamont would never have written a line like this: "He goes, rubbing the muscular loins that he batters." First of all because the line is not very beautiful and then because the swelling does not render the strangely inverted stretching, a relaxation through internal contraction that fills with a sluggishness one knows to be ephemeral and without danger.

Failing to return to the origins of animal actions in the nerves, de Lisle cannot give the creatures in his bestiary much individuality. In short there is not much difference between the black panther and the jaguar. Their leaps are not described in terms of their precise cruelty. They are no more than abstract parabolas.

When de Lisle reinforces his animals, he does so with *adjectives* without living out their verbal action, understanding the specific will behind it or testing the analytic values of anger and cruelty. Thus a stallion becomes *carnivorous*, like Diomedes' horses, through a merely literary device. De Lisle has never witnessed the strange look of a biting horse.

Conversely the bear *roars* in the *Poèmes barbares*, though legends simply say that it growls. As a matter of fact a medieval legend states, "God passed by and someone or other growled. God changed him into a bear so that he could growl when he wished." A black tower would also *roar* when it fell. The *Poèmes barbares* are full of such roars, surges, bristling hair and hoarse cries—a whole poetry of ra-re-ri-ro-ru, coarse as a syllabary, more raging than enraged, crumbling suddenly into a landslide of adverbs and substantives ending in -ly and -ing.

> Pale hair in thick windings
> Crackled in shadows horribly;
> And behind, in rough, long hummings
> There unreeled, according to species and size,
> The animals of the earth and of the heavenly circlings.

Sometimes a petrified phrase disturbs the suppleness of movements and contradicts the direct truth of impulsion. Lautréamont the swimmer would never have written a line like this one: "In the wave where fish lacerate their white *loins*," for the fish is above all a *lateral energy*. It swims by moving its sides, and its tail is only the place where they converge. Man, on the contrary, swims with a vertical energy by using his loins. Side and breaststrokes are auxiliaries. With so much needed to translate animal phenomenology faithfully, the swimming would have to be rather heroic if the fish are to lacerate their *loins*. But Leconte de Lisle simply could not resist the easy temptation of empty and sonorous energy in an extra "*l.*"

De Lisle sticks monsters, summas of fiery metamorphoses in Lautréamont, into traditional shells. Echidna, "Daughter of Chrysaor and Callirhoe" (if I may be allowed, for a moment, to play with the alexandrine and merge the coagulation of "c" sounds), Echidna, "Enormous half-reptile with scales on her belly," is ultimately only a digesting monster that devours her lovers—the most ordinary of psychoanalytical symbols—bones and all. She does not possess that conspicuous violence of fresh misdeeds, Ducassian misdeeds.

I have carefully worked out the bestiary of *Poémes barbares*. The number of animals mentioned is 113. The repetitions of animal forms are fewer than in *Maldoror*, so I can state generally that the animal density is half what it is in Lautréamont. Moreover this animality is much less intense. Often it has been vanquished and stuffed. The giant wolf has been conquered and turned into an enormous carpet or bedside rug. Sometimes there appears "an old, resigned tiger that a child leads on a leash."[3] Because it is huge the hippopotamus is described as short-winded. This is the law of human, all too human, diagnostics. Hunters, as representatives of the middle class, hunt in order to supply "rich banquets." Ganders and peacocks, symbols of pride and vanity, are roasted indiscriminately. Beasts are named for the sake of rhymes: an auroch because it rhymes with "roc," according to the law of hard sonorities. The ear, that passive organ, governs those elements (ignoring all hierarchy) that come from the poetry of energy. Innumerable absurdities are the result in de Lisle. Animal life becomes a platitude expressed in lifeless verse: "If a fierce animal is hungry and thirsty, let him eat!"[4]

3. Leconte de Lisle, *Poèmes barbares* (Paris, 1952), 159.
4. Ibid., 130.

Birds flock from the islands to display their colors; waxbill, cardinal, hummingbird are a blur of sapphire and ruby. The animals are distinguished by adjectives that characterize them poorly. That is never the case with Lautréamont. The eagle is white or black without reason. Sometimes de Lisle amasses animals in the matrix of an alexandrine without being able to make them live: "Bats, owls, wyverns, flying dragons."[5] Nevertheless, I should point out on the same page an animal fusion of the Ducassian variety that in my opinion justifies my diagnostics of the complex:

> And I have seen in nocturnal shadows,
> The silent birds gather into a whole,
> Melting closely together as though one
> Hideous beast possessing the ugliness of each,
> Spider with teeth and claws, green
> As a Nile dragon, with foam covered,
> A foam of mute fury, and with the pleasure
> That comes from spoiling for others what he cannot seize.

But this fusion leaves behind too much residue. Nightmare dragons, aggregates of teeth and paws, swollen with tongues, are never "Nile dragons." They swim in unnamed waters. The rhythm interrupts the poetic elevation; inversions that are needed for rhyme, such as "with foam covered," muddle the visions. Such a passage, tinged with didacticism, does not have the hallucinatory qualities that are so palpable in Flaubert's *The Temptation of St. Anthony.* Despite his pursuit of sound effects, Flaubert can paint images of scarlet over the pure ebony of night by dreaming accurately: "I have lived in that shapeless world where hermaphroditic animals dozed . . . in the depths of dim waters—when fingers, fins and wings were mixed together and eyes without a head floated like mollusks among bulls with human faces and snakes with the feet of dogs."[6]

In more straightforward impulses, such as those that rise from anger to insult, the animalizations created by Leconte

5. Ibid., 331–32.
6. Gustave Flaubert, *The Temptation of Saint Anthony*, Trans. Lafcadio Hearn (New York, 1911), 179. Cf. 16.

de Lisle are better. They rediscover naturally the traditional synthesis of contradictory attitudes, a synthesis of opening and closing mouths executed by the barking dog and hissing snake, "And I will punish you in your flesh and breed,/O viper, O jackal, son and father of dogs!"[7]

But these insults wrought after traditional models cannot match the vigor of primal insult, and despite a few fine lines the psychological force subsides. In the end a psychology of complexes can disclose only schemas and outlines, not impulses and forces, in the work of this Parnassian poet.

Need I say it? Naturally my criticism applies only to the level of psychological dynamics. I am not unaware of some beautiful lines and passages. Incidentally, I find admirable among the category of images we are studying: "The Nepal tiger that smells the antelope."[8] I listen perplexed to the noises of shadows: "Where, in dismal nights, the cayman whines."[9]

I still maintain my schoolboy admiration for poems like "The Elephants," "The Sleep of the Condor," and "The Black Panther." These are masterpieces of painting, of sculpted poetry that allow us, as Albert Thibaudet so rightly says, to place Leconte de Lisle among the "animalists." Any historian of poetry would recognize them as successful illustrations, well suited to the taste of their times, fully established within a solid aesthetic community that is sure of its constitution. Poetic revolution is something else. Lautréamont is a risk.

IV

I shall confine myself to two examples of complexual explication in the realm of literary criticism. I have chosen them to be as different as possible, the first an almost conscious arrangement of the theme, the second with a more muted thrust and completely unconscious. A reader familiar with

7. Leconte de Lisle, *Poèmes barbares*, 35.
8. Ibid., 138.
9. Ibid., 187.

the works of Leconte de Lisle will perhaps be repelled by such an explication, but I would ask him to assume the burden of proof and explain for himself the accumulation of animal references, the consciously sought severity, the deliberate harshness, the rough echoes of primitive life in the *Poèmes barbares*—in short the whole sophisticated legend of primitivity, presented without the least objective support. He would have to answer that one cannot subscribe to the uncouth emotions of the *Poèmes barbares* or pursue the weighty hypothesis of Wells except in the company of certain reveries or through a childish return to the origins of life, to a brutish origin in which we think that a young and terrifying power can always be grasped anew. The most sensitive man, the man most tempered by life, at certain times dreams of the un-tamed. He respects, admires, loves the power that defies him. To understand violence in a permissible way—in a minor key—within the already airy life of ideas, is, for a philosopher, to practice it. To *understand* violence is to provide violence with the moral guarantee of idealism. There is thus a platonic violence, one stranger still than platonic love. These philosophers do not hunt, they read *Le Runoia*: "Hunters of bears and wolves, stand up, O my warriors."

To sum up, if there are in poems about the primitive a cause for conviction, an attraction, a charm, their source would not be in the seductiveness of objective images—in the precise memory or in reminiscences of a faraway past. These poems are as ignorant of historical as they are of objective reality. They can take on their synthesizing power only in an unconscious complex, one so hidden from what we know of ourselves that in explicating it we believe we have discovered a reality.

V

But since I have indicted the naïve realism of animality in this fashion, I must ask if the first attempts at scientific objectivity were better controlled, if they avoided the primal seduction of the Lautréamont complex. It seems not. In the animal kingdom more than any other natural realm, common sense clings to its primal ideas, its first errors, and it hampers positive knowledge for a long time. This is the reason for the unbelievable precepts that get in the way of *medical matters* and lead to the use of particular remedies drawn from the animal kingdom.

Moreover, we never change our opinions about an animal because it is from the very first classified among either the dangerous or the harmless. Knowledge is in this instance more clearly than anywhere else a *function of fear*. Knowledge of an animal is thus the balance sheet of the respective human and animal aggressions. The first image is the concretizing of a first emotion. C. G. Jung has noted that it "is almost impossible to escape the power of primordial images."[10] Now the animal is among the strongest of archetypes. We should not be surprised by the profound induration of animal phobias.

A complete classification of animal phobias and philias would yield a sort of *affective animal kingdom* that would be interesting to compare with the *animal kingdom* described in the bestiaries of antiquity and the Middle Ages. In both cases —in vesanias and in bestiaries—we would see that objective values are also rare; and in both, affective polarization is just as clear.

We could then emphasize the proximity, increasingly narrower day by day, between psychiatry and animal psychology. In fact Korzybski has recently shown that animal psychology could illustrate the majority of diatheses uncovered by psychiatry. Thus malformations of the human imagination fall back into real animal forms. The fine work of H.

10. Carl Gustave Jung, *The Relations Between the Ego and the Unconscious*, in *Two Essays on Analytical Psychology*, trans. R. F. C. Hull (*Collected Works* 7) (New York, 1953), 234.

Baruk on animal experimentation in psychiatry would offer innumerable arguments in support of this thesis.[11]

We should perhaps go even further and openly suggest the reciprocal side of the preceding thesis. We would then be led to declare that *the animal is an alien* or, again forcing the point to make it more evident, that the various animal species are different forms of mental alienation. There is a reason: animals are subject to a specific vital determinism. They are not "mechanical contrivances," but they are more precisely the playthings of a contrived animality. Instinct is a mono-mania, and every monomania conceals a specific instinct. The quickest way to describe a human aberration is to com-pare it with animal behavior. The animal is a monovalent psychic state.

At the other extreme lies the human. It is given in the fine definition proposed by André Gide: "I used to call man the animal capable of a gratuitous action." A truly human cure would give the lie to the instincts; it would be a liberation from all forms of animalizing alienation. As a consequence action would have to go through a period of inhibition to be truly considered specifically human. Perhaps an effective training for that inhibition would be to deploy the instincts in a kind of counterpoint by putting some aggression into tenderness, for instance, or a certain pity into the holocaust. Then affectivity would produce a multiplicity of many-col-ored flowers.

This slight sketch of a thesis that I cannot develop at more length in this short book will perhaps be enough to present the problem of Lautréamont's "madness" in a clearer light and bring together opposing theories. It is first of all quite evident that an attachment to animal life undertaken so will-ingly must give the reader a definite impression of frenzy. But in *Maldoror* there is such a variety of frenzies and a power of

11. Cf. Alfred Korzybski, *Science and sanity: An introduction to non-Aristotelian systems and general semantics* (Lancaster, Pa. & New York: 1933), 362, and Henri Baruk, *Psychiatrie médicale, physiologique et expérimentale: semeiologie, thérapeutique* (Paris, 1938).

metamorphosis that the breaking of instincts, in my opinion, has been achieved. I have pointed out that *Maldoror* also contains experiences of suspended action, delayed threats, deferred behavior—in short, tokens not only of a kinetic but also of a genuinely potential psychic state. Thus it seems that Lautréamont has doubly escaped the fatality of actions and that his strange, fiery thought remains that of a human mind which has mastered itself.

If this deduction is correct, we may see the reciprocal illustration in Lautréamontism of Gide's gratuitousness. This illustration is even clearer because the lines are so enlarged and simplified. It seems that the pattern of actions in Lautréamont can follow only a straight line. Gide's gratuitousness is more supple; it bends everything, even impulses. Thus it reveals an inner richness in gestures that is quite different from their ostensible wealth. To put it another way, gratuitousness remains external to existence when it appears in Lautréamont, while for Gide it is truly integrated into being. But at the end apprenticeship to gratuitousness will take its first lessons from *Maldoror*. From the first, André Gide has been a maldororan.[12]

I may perhaps be criticized for having emphasized too heavily the deviations produced by the imagination in creating the medieval bestiaries. In fact there is a reciprocal action between the naive imagination and animal images. Bestiaries look childish because, from the first, childrearing is so attached to them. City children receive toy animals among their first playthings. Their first books are often veritable bestiaries. Someone has asked if the famous *sonnet on the vowels* was not a reflection of the colored ABC book of Arthur Rimbaud. Could an animalized ABC have forever influenced Isidore Ducasse as well?

Whatever may be the answer, it is certain that the problem of verbal culture must be individualized. We should see that the relation between first impressions and first words, first

12. Cf. Larbaud, "Lautréamont et Laforgue," *loc. cit.*

complexes and first tropes, is much closer than we have imagined and that as a result poetry in its primitive verbal function is deeply engraved in certain special souls. Poetry is then revealed as a natural psychic syncretism that is reproduced in certain experiences of endophasia and automatic writing. Primitive poetry is always a profound psychological experience.[13]

13. Cf. Jean Cazaux, *Surréalisme et Psychologie: Endophaisie et écriture automatique* (Paris, 1938), *passim.*

Conclusion

I

BY PURSUING A very specific branch of poetic evolution, we
have just seen that a series of well-defined poetic states continues throughout its development. They all bear the stamp
of a very special psychological reality. If this rough sketch
were continued and completed, it seems to me that a real *line
of force* for the imagination would be disclosed. This line of
force would take its point of departure from a truly vital pole
that is deeply inscribed in living matter. It would proceed
through a world of living forms *executed* in well-defined
bestiaries, then through a zone of *trial* forms—experimental
dreams, to use Tristan Tzara's phrase—to end finally in a
more or less clear awareness of the almost anarchic freedom
of spiritualization. All along this line of force we would sense
the richness of living matter. According to its stage of metamorphosis, we would see mute life on fire, definite life attack-
ing, dream life in play and thought.

Such a *line of force* seems to be capable of synthesizing two
fine philosophic works, each different from the other, which
have recently renewed the doctrine of creative imagination:
Imagination and Realization by Armand Petitjean and *Myth
and Man* by Roger Caillois. These two works throw new light
on the biological character of the imagination and consequently on the vital necessity for poetry. Along with the two
dialectical principles of the internal coordination of forms
and the uncoordinated play of ornamentation, poetry is thus
the dominant factor in evolution.

Without claiming to summarize in a few pages books that
must be read pen in hand, I shall show in what perspective I

see them and also how I am bending their lines to meet my own reflections. Then we shall recognize how the axis of Lautréamontism helps us to sketch the line of force that represents life's aesthetic endeavor.

II

Roger Caillois, it seems to me, holds the record for descent into living reality, while Armand Petitjean, at the other pole of biological poetry, reveals the most deeply hidden conditions of these new vital achievements.

Caillois takes us down into the maelstrom of life to the very center of the eddy that dynamizes biological evolution. Approaching this pole we see that a living being has an *appetite for forms* at least as great as his *appetite for matter*. The living being, whoever he may be, must bring diverse forms into solidarity, live through a transformation, accept metamorphoses, display a truly acting, powerfully dynamic formal causality. There must be a certain point by point correspondence among the different formal trajectories—that is, among the forms that run through different beings characterized by a specific formal becoming. At this point Caillois' fundamental equation between man and animal is presented: "Here behavior, there mythology."[1] What unifies the actions of an insect in his behavior unites the beliefs of man in a mythology. An extensive study of projective poetry must succeed in *projecting* animal behavior on human mythology.

This equality of animal behavior and human myth has a function utterly different from Bergson's now classic parallel between instinct and intelligence. In fact both work under the impulsion of external necessity, while behavior and myths appear as more of an inner destiny. Thus, being acts *against* reality and is no longer equated with it. Aggressive behavior and cruel myths are both functions of attack, dynamizing principles. They sharpen being. It is not simply a matter of knowing what to do either on the level of behavior

1. Roger Caillois, *Le Mythe et l'Homme* (Paris, 1938), 31.

or of myth. One must *will* to do, must have the energy to do. Devouring surpasses assimilating, or better, one only assimilates completely what one devours.

On this level of violence we always discover a pure, gratuitous beginning, an instant of aggression, a Ducassean moment. Aggression is unforeseeable as much for the attacker as for the attacked. This is one of the clearest lessons to be drawn from the study of Lautréamont.

This aggression, controlled by a Ducassean instant, is found both in the instinct and in the intelligence. Cruelty must be placed at the origin of instinct; without it *animal behavior* cannot begin. The lowest creature, the most innocent butterfly at the most beautiful flower cannot unfold its probe without a gesture of attack. But intelligence must also be *corrosive*. It *attacks* a problem. If it can solve it, the result is placed in memory, in organization, but insofar as it really organizes, the intelligence aggresses, it transforms. A lively intelligence is served by a lively look and by lively words. Sooner or later it must wound. Intelligence is always a factor of surprise, of stratagem. It is a hypocritical force. It attacks resolutely only after a thousand ruses. Intelligence is a graft that breaks while being peeled off.

And so—especially if we emphasize the initial phase of aggression a little—Caillois' equation leads us to the idea that a *pure act* must desire a form, a coherence, a total success that is already guaranteed by the initial aggression. The pure act, then, totally separated from the passive functions of simple defense, is a *poeticizing* in every sense of the word. It makes for behavior in the animal and myth in primitive man. Pierre Janet has very rightly esteemed the inaugural phase that puts all ceremonies into a purified time and removes them from daily life, that thrusts a poetry on them, that provides in an instant a supremacy of formal over efficient cause. By studying the book of Armand Petitjean we shall see that the pure act establishes art and science in their newness and that accordingly the relationship of imagination and will is closer than we generally think. In any event I have said enough about the thesis of Roger Caillois to make it clear that it is possible to see in it an extrapolation of Ducassean impulses, a prolongation of the Ducasse axis on the side of biological values. This zone of primitive life is extremely rich and diverse. As I have hinted earlier,[2] the bestiary of our dreams animates a life that returns to biological depths. The sexual symbolism of classical psychoanalysis is only one aspect of the problem. All the functions can create symbols; all biological heresies can produce phantasms. Caillois discovers and explores an infrared of the life of the passions whose extent was undreamed of before *Myth and Man*.

Conversely it seems to me that Lautréamontism brings out in somewhat too exaggerated a fashion the vital poeticizing forces revealed by Caillois. With Lautréamont in fact poetry is candidly set in a clear dynamism as a need for action, a will to take advantage of all living forms in order to give their action a poetic character, their formal causality. But Ducassean *behavior* is *launched* rather than *pursued*. It ends by losing the flexibility of real behavior as well as the affection of poetic behavior. It is so precipitous and so straightforward that it cannot take on all the delicate entreaties that poetic myth succeeds in integrating into the animal behavior that is its foundation. It is understandable, then, that Ducasse's poetry, full of an abundant, vigorous power, has a decidedly inhuman character and will not allow us to bring about a harmonious synthesis between the dark forces and the disciplined forces of our being.

III

Let us now move on to the other pole of the line of force going through the vital imagination. We shall see how Armand Petitjean discovers and explores the ultraviolet end of a life of clarity. We shall also see how, in regard to Lautréamontism, we must face another extrapolation. From the first it seems

2. Cf. *supra*, 9.

that we must struggle against the mediocrity of our psychological life, that we must break down images and behavior to find the *res novae* within and without us. The maneuvers of Ducasse's disobedience seem quite insufficient, the actions energized by animal imitations too few when we have understood Petitjean's disobedience. As soon as it is free, the value of clarity activates the imagination and moves it from imitation to creation. Petitjean sees that the imagination will no longer be merely equal to whatever has already happened in the past. The past of the real, of perception, of memory—the world and dreams—gives us only images to destroy and smash. The imagination then becomes equal to a future. Petitjean's image is not, in my opinion, an object of sight but of foresight. To foresee is always to imagine. Imagination must caress the lightly sculpted forms of the near future. It must provide an energy chart for distinguishing what resists from what yields. It gathers ripe fruit, the finished form with its fuzz and juice. Forms are the *decisive* instants of formal causality. And in contemplating Petitjean's book we can easily rediscover Ducasse's teachings and paradoxes. The decisive instants of formal causality are the instants in which forms are transformed, in which metamorphosis provides the complete range of existence.

Since it is the imagination, essentially, that foresees, poetry would once again take up its prophetic role if that role had not given occasion to such obvious abuses. In fact the prophetic character of new thought does not come from a Pythian spirit; it is both more natural and more rational. We shall not ask the poet to give us Huysmans's "bellowing secrets"; secrets are no longer internal, sensual or buried in the past, for all past times are alike. Rather, secrets are formal, mathematical, projected as perfectly coherent signs into a well-constructed future.

However, no more than Lautréamont does Petitjean propose a distant transcendence. For him, foreseeing is immanent within seeing. We can only see well if we foresee a bit, and so a psycho-physiological contemplation of vision would offer a *psychics of nature* while a meditation on the objectivity of knowledge of the real offered a *physics of thought*.[3] More briefly, we could say that images and imagination are as closely united as action and reaction in the realm of forces. We grasp "the mutual obligation between object and subject, the object requiring the subject in order to be freed from itself in imagination—its fulfillment—and the object taking the place of the subject as the hinge over which imagination folds, forever abolishing its randomness."[4]

Thus the gratuitousness of actions is delicately managed. The formal cause masters the accident of the picturesque without overwhelming it. By detaching himself from it so abruptly, Lautréamont seemed to destroy behavior arbitrarily, but he always submitted to one mode of behavior. He was thus the plaything of his playthings, the slave of his means of freedom. Petitjean does not fall into this error. He coordinates his freedoms. He understands that we cannot determine actions by impulsions, courage by mere speed. Put another way, imagining cannot be pure kineticism. One cannot fall completely under its spell in the joy of acting without goals. Young and eager philosopher that he is, Petitjean truly wants the imagination to *fulfill*. It is only through fulfillment that imagination can have convergence.

But in the world of images fulfillment does not demand domination like efficient causes; the mind, in its imagining activity, will be unburdened of the weight of things. Above all what must be mastered is formal cause. Imagination must avoid having formal causes pursue the catagenetic fate that somehow allows forms through some peculiar inertia to stiffen, grow dull and wear out like tufa eroded by moss, betrayed within by its porous and loose substance. The mind must rediscover the youthfulness of form, the vigor—or

3. In "Le Moderne et son prochain," ch. 13 of Armand Petitjean's *Imagination et Réalisation*, the author presents some of the topics of his next work. Cf. in particular the uniting of a physics of thought with a psychics of nature.
4. Petitjean, *Imagination et Réalisation*, 68.

rather joy—of formal causality. It must trace the growth of beauty when the innocence of a glance is transformed into tenderness. Finally, in the fullness of age the mind must attain a vibrant formal causality that develops its projects in every direction.

Thus we arrive at a *poetry of the project* that truly *opens up* the imagination. The past, the real, the dream itself give us only a closed imagination, since they have at their disposal only a group of predetermined images. But with the open imagination there appears a sort of *myth of hope* that is symmetrical with the *myth of memory*. Or, rather, hope is the vague, ordinary, impoverished impression that colors the future of a man half blind. Another light is borne by the doctrine of active imagination. The *project*—otherwise stated, formal hope, which aims for its own form—is quite different from the project that has a form in view as the token of some desired reality, some reality condensed into matter. Forms are not tokens but genuine realities. The *pure imagination* designates its projected forms as the essence of its proper fulfillment. It delights naturally in imagining, thus in changing forms. Metamorphosis thus becomes the specific function of imagination. The imagination cannot comprehend a form except by transforming it, by dynamizing its becoming, by seizing on it like a sectioning of the flux of formal causality, precisely as a physicist cannot understand a phenomenon except by grasping it in a sectioning of the flux of efficient causality.

IV

If these views can be accepted, then one can realize that the fiery, brutal metamorphoses of Lautréamont do not resolve the central problem of poetry, for these metamorphoses were obliged to take on the efficient causality of natural gestures. But Ducasse's metamorphoses have had the advantage of unanchoring a type of poetry submerged in the job of describing. In my opinion we must now take advantage of a life given over to the metamorphosing powers in order to move on to a sort of *non-Lautréamontism* that will spill out of *Maldoror* in all directions. I shall continue to use the term "non-Lautréamontism" while giving it the same function as that non-Euclideanism which can generalize Euclidean geometry. It is not a question of *opposing* Lautréamontism in any way but of awakening certain dialectics on the most fruitful levels of Ducassean principles.

It is in the reintegration of the human into the passionate life that we see first step in this non-Lautréamontism. The question to be asked is as follows: "How can one bring about truly human, anagenetic, *open* metamorphoses?" The way of direct human exertion is only a poor extension of animal exertion. It is in the *dream of action* that the truly human joy of action resides. To cause to act without acting; to leave bound time for liberated time, performance time for decision time, the ponderously continuous time of functions for the dazzling time of a moment of projection; to replace a philosophy of action, too often a philosophy of agitation, with a philosophy of repose and then a philosophy of the consciousness of reposing, solitude and reserve power—such are the preliminary tasks for a pedagogy of the imagination. Next, this repose of the imagination must be taken as the point of departure for a discovery of firmly deanimalized thought-motifs, free from all allurement, cut off from the hypnotism of images, clearly separated from the *categories* of understanding that are concretized forms of intellectual prudence, "fossilized states of intellectual repression." Then the imagination will be back in its function of testing, risking, being imprudent, creating.

Then the mind is free for the *metaphor of metaphor*. It is with this concept that I ended my recent book *The Psychoanalysis of Fire*. I did not undertake this long meditation on the work of Lautréamont with the goal of writing a *psychoanalysis of life*. In the end to resist images of fire or those of life is the same thing. A doctrine that resists primal images, those images already created, already formed, already taught, must also resist primal metaphors. It must also choose: should one burn with fire, break with life, or continue with life? For me the choice has been made. The new poetry and ideas demand a breaking off and a conversion. Life must desire thought. No value is specifically human if it is not the result of a renunciation and a conversion. A specifically human value is always a *converted* natural value. Lautréamontism, the result of a primal dynamization, appears to me as a value to be converted, as a power of expansion to be transformed. Intellectual values must be grafted onto Lautréamontism. These values will receive a corrosiveness, an audacity, a prodigality—in short everything needed to give us a good conscience, a joy of abstracting, a joy of being man.

By pursuing my non-Lautréamontian interpretation of Lautréamontism, we shall doubtless lose all the joys of wrath, but we shall preserve the charms of alertness. At any rate a reader of *Maldoror*, once he has lived through the poetry of aggression in a vigorous form, will never forget its tonic power. Lautréamont places poetry in the nerve centers. He projects poetry without any intermediary. He uses the *present tense* of words. From this simple linguistic point of view he was already ahead of his contemporaries, poets who for the most part lived a history of language, spoke a classical phonetics, and restated, like Leconte de Lisle, echoes often powerless and always unconvincing of the heroic voices of the past.

Endnotes

The author's original notes, corrected when necessary, have been kept in place at the bottom of the page. All other information or commentary on the translation has been assembled in these endnotes. They are referenced neither by means of superscripts in the text nor by page and line numbers but by page and key. This key consists of the beginning word or phrase of the line in which the reference occurs. The reader can locate a keyword in the text by scanning the first words at the left margin. For instance, bibliographical information for the reference on page two to "pure poetry" is keyed to "gression in" at the beginning of line ten. If a quotation occupies more than one line, the final line is the one referenced.

P. 1   **The Vigorous Poetry of Aggression**: in the French, "Agression et poésie nerveuse" (Aggression and Vigorous Poetry). The adjective "nerveux" means "vigorous," "forceful," "snappy," "lively," and "responsive."
       Live with such speed: Could not be located in Emmanuel E. Signoret's *Poésies complètes*. Bachelard may have found it in Signoret's unfinished novel, *Jacinthus*, several chapters of which were published in *Revue Sentimentale*, *Mercure de France*, and *Syrinx*, or in one of his essays ("Essais d'art libre" and "Essai sur l'Italie, sur Ronsard et sur Goethe").
       Man can bear: John Cowper Powys, *Wolf Solent* (Garden City, N. Y.: Garden City Publishing Co., 1933), 887.
       things meet in time : in the French, "liaisons temporelles."
       Maldoror: *Les chants de Maldoror* by Le Comte de Lautréamont, the pseudonym of Isidore Ducasse, has been translated several times, in whole or in part, into English. The best version to date is by Alexis Lykiard, *Lautréamont's Maldoror* (New York: Thomas V. Crowell, 1972). As the translator points out, "*chant* in French suggests not merely 'song,' but also 'canto,' 'epic,' and 'lay.' Nesselroth has noted the Orphic elements implicit in the title, and it seems to me that Rodker, for once, is apt in selecting 'lay.' Contemporary readers, however, may be misled by the word's unfortunate slang connotation, and thus my translation simply (and chastely) invokes the name of its ubiquitous yet elusive protag-

onist" (Appendix B, 214). The same practice is followed, for the sake of simplicity, in this translation of Bachelard's book and in the accompanying essays. Lautréamont's prose poem is referred to as *Maldoror*, in italics, as distinguished from the protagonist Maldoror. "Chant" is translated as "canto."

Maxime Alexandre: The source for this citation could not be identified. Alexandre was the author of a collection of free verse, *Le corsage* (Paris, 1931) and a *Mythologie personnelle* (Paris, 1933).

P. 2   **Second, I**: for the term "complex" see below, Hillman, 109.

gression in: "pure poetry" refers to the celebrated book of Henri Bremond, *La poésie pure* (Paris, 1926).

attack. La: The fables are among the most familiar of seventeenth-century French poetic classics, known and often memorized from an early age by every school child. Bachelard's comparison of La Fontaine with Ducasse suggests not so much a criticism of a standard author as a rejection of the canons of French classicism in favor of the "new poetry" emanating from Lautréamont.

P. 3   **biting. Here**: "will-to-live" suggests not only the vitalistic philosophies of the nineteenth century but especially the evolutionary optimism of Bergson, whom Bachelard criticizes later in this chapter.

mont, how: The allusion to Nietzsche comes from *Thus Spake Zarathustra*, in *The Portable Nietzsche*, Trans. and ed. Walter Kaufmann (New York, 1976), 121: "For ten years you have climbed to my cave: you would have tired of your light and of the journey had it not been for my eagle and my serpent."

My own investigation: The Corti text is frequently reprinted. Comte de Lautréamont (Isidore Ducasse), *Oeuvres complètes: Les Chants de Maldoror, Poésies, Lettres* (Paris, 1953). Citations from Lautréamont in the text represent fresh translations from the original French. However, in this commentary and in the footnotes they are keyed, for the reader's convenience, to Alexis Lykiard's translation and to the Corti text. The first page number refers to the Lykiard translation and the second, in parentheses, to the Corti edition.

P. 4   **works of Victor**: the once popular *Les travailleurs de la mer* has been translated into English numerous times. Cf. Victor Hugo, *The Toilers of the Sea* (London & New York, 1931).

camellias": *Maldoror* 85 (220)

and the anemone: *Maldoror* 92 (229)

niums" is *Maldoror* 91 (227)

P. 5   **the rose-beetle:** According to Paul Lespès, as reported by François Alicot (and cited by Philippe Soupault, Corti edition, 55), "He was much interested in natural history. The animal world vividly excited his curiosity. I once saw him contemplate at length a brilliant red rose-beetle that he had found in the school park during the noon recess."
"almost impeccable: In the Corti edition, page 25.
Jean Cassou: "La cote actuelle de Lautréamont," in *Isidore Ducasse, comte de Lautréamont, Le Cas Lautréamont, Etudes, notes et opinions inédites de Marcel Arland, C. Arnauld, A. Breton . . .* Editions du "Disque vert" (Paris-Brussels, 1925).

P. 6   **In his** *Epistle* : Giacomo Girolamo Casanova de Seingalt, *Lena Caprina, lettre d'un lycanthrope* (Paris, 1926).
frenzy and especially: "bonheur" (happiness) is translated here as "bliss."
contemplated my: *Maldoror* 130 (272)
it night after: *Maldoror* 131 (274)
right, of: *Maldoror* 131 (274)

P. 7   **move a chest:** Kafka's original German text has "viertelstündiger," "a quarter of an hour's" work rather than "four hours." A few pages earlier, however, Gregor requires four hours to pull a sheet over the sofa.
shaking his head: This passage describes Gregor's father rather than Gregor.
whom he wooed: Kafka, 69.

P. 11   **arguments and:** *Maldoror* 132 (275)
slender as a: *Maldoror* 132 (275)
"an untameable: *Maldoror* 135 (279)

P. 12   **earthworm:** *Maldoror* 133 (276)
criterion: *Maldoror* 133 (276)

P. 13   **Alfred de Vigny:** *Stello: A Session with Doctor Noir*, trans. Irving Massey (Montreal, 1963), 46.
The horse and: 'Teratological'—that is, concerning stories about monsters, attracted to the monstrous or contemplative of monstrosities.

P. 14   **tion—"As:** *Maldoror* 3 (125)

P. 16   **"in his oblique:** *Maldoror* 9 (132)

P. 17   **obsession of:** *Maldoror* 23 (148)
foot . . . as: *Maldoror* 53 (183)
only its steel: *Maldoror* 82 (216)
claws in my: *Maldoror* 82 (217)

out claw against: *Maldoror* 88 (224)
nails grow for: *Maldoror* 4 (127)
The Ocean itself: *Maldoror* 17 (141)

P. 19   **branches."**: *Maldoror* 44 (173)
The penknife: *Maldoror* 94 (230)
variety called: The tourteau is a species of edible Atlantic crab.
steps?" The: *Maldoror* 29 (155)

P. 20   **like blades of:** *Maldoror* 54 (185)
esteem above the: *Maldoror* 55 (185)
your way, move: *Maldoror* 56 (186)
not the louse: *Maldoror* 55 (185)
liberator, you: *Maldoror* 57 (187)
growth of your: *Maldoror* 57 (187)
angel wings 59 (190)

P. 21   **commit this crime:** *Maldoror* 6 (129)
is necessary: *Maldoror* 96 (232)
tremendous leaps: *Maldoror* 97 (232)

P. 22   **old spider:** *Maldoror* 164 (312)
suction.": *Maldoror* 165 (313)
spider and come: *Maldoror* 166 (315)
. . ." The: *Maldoror* 12 (136)
screech horribly: *Maldoror* 81 (215)

P. 23   **to take a:** *Maldoror* 81 (215)
"science.": Bachelard does not indicate his exact source.
that became: *Maldoror* 82 (215-16)

P. 24   **with its belly:** *Maldoror* 164 (312-13)
him: "Why: *Maldoror* 36 (163)
Jeanne Mégnen: A published source for this poem could not be located.
winged octopi: *Maldoror* 80 (213)
clings to the: *Maldoror* 97 (234)

P. 25   **female shark :** *Maldoror* 10 (134)
face to face: *Maldoror* 77 (211)
coals. How : *Maldoror* 89 (225)

P. 26   **amorality and:** *Maldoror* 108 (247)
ness? Must we: Nicolas-Sébastien Roch de Chamfort (1741-1794), author of a book of rather savage *Maxims*.
Ducasse's volucrary: A coinage based on Latin *volucris*, "flying creature," and "bestiary."

P. 27   **took flight:** *Maldoror* 201 (354)

P. 28   **The invitation:** Bachelard is alluding to Baudelaire's famous poem.

This notion: The word "primitif" in French means both "primitive" and "primal" in English. As Bachelard uses the term, it sometimes means one or the other or both.

P. 30   **compare with Baudelaire's**: In his well-known sonnet "Correspondences."

P. 32   **vermin, the furrows**: In French, "Ces mines de vermines, ces fosses à poux, cette purulence qui pullule. . . ."

P. 33   **Léon-Paul Fargue**: "Colère," in *Espaces*, *Poésies* (Paris, 1963), 176. The poem concerns the inability to recapture the music of words. Bachelard's citation of it as epigraph to this chapter suggests the schoolboy's anger and frustration in his rhetoric class.

P. 34   **understanding.''**: *Maldoror* 1 (124)

      specific complexes: The word "culturel" in French means both "pertaining to culture" and "pertaining to education."

P. 35   **sions, cuts out**: *Oeuvres complètes*, 381.

      recursion point: In mathematics, recursion refers to the defining of a value, after a first case is given, by repeated references back to the previously established value. What Bachelard is describing is the way that what one learns in his first experience of formal linguistic education continues to shape and be reshaped by one's subsequent practice.

P. 36   **at a man**: *Maldoror* 5 (128)

      blood and tears: *Maldoror* 5 (128)

      plague victim: *Maldoror* 26 (152)

P. 37   **ability to express**: *Maldoror* 126 (268)

      exact period of: *Maldoror* 128 (271)

      apparent in: *Maldoror* 126 (267)

      head, polished: *Maldoror* 138 (283)

      Sarcey's letter: Francisque Sarcey (1827-1899), a prolific writer and critic. Bachelard is perhaps reflecting on his own academic position and his luxuriant mane and beard.

P. 38   **real man**: Wells, *The Island of Dr. Moreau*, 148 (see above, p. 72, footnote 2, for the full reference).

P. 40   **contempt.''**: *Maldoror* 81 (215)

P. 41   **the wind for**: This description of Rimbaud comes from Paul Verlaine. See "L'homme aux semelles de vent," in the Introduction of Suzanne Bernard to her edition of Arthur Rimbaud, *Oeuvres* (Paris, 1960), lxiii.

P. 43   **René Char**, *Moulin premier*, XVII, in *Oeuvres complètes* (Paris, 1983), 68-69. Char's poem tells of a woman who is taken for dead but comes suddenly back to life and gains a vivid awareness of her interior animality.

P. 44   **would be to**: Paul Schilder, *The Image and Appearance of the Human Body; Studies in the Constructive Energies of the Psyche* (1935; rpr. New York, 1950). Henry Head, author of *The Sense of Stability and Balance in the Air* (London, 1919), *Studies in Neurology,* 2 vols. (London, 1920), and *Aphasia and Kindred Disorders of Speech,* 2 vols. (Cambridge, 1926).

           studied by: Jacques Jean Lhermitte, *L'image de notre corps* (Paris, 1939).

P. 45   **every function**: "dynamogenic," meaning increasing mental and motor activity by stimulating a sense organ.

P. 47   **though driven**: See Edmond Jaloux, "Note sur les Chants de Maldoror," in *Le Cas Lautréamont.*

           work. "You: *Oeuvres complètes* 400

P. 48   **polemical impulse**: *Oeuvres complètes* 368

           be born: *Oeuvres complètes* 363

           keep it to : *Oeuvres complètes* 372

P. 49   **This is likewise** Gil Robin, "Le comte de Lautréamont n'habite pas un asile, mais un palais," in *Le Cas Lautréamont.*

           tivity, Painlevé: Paul Painlevé was a mathematician and socialist-republican politician whose main research was in analysis and mechanics. He was Président du Conseil in 1917 and 1925.

P. 51   **honey, filtered**: *Maldoror* 59 (190)

P. 52   **and modesty**: *Maldoror* 61 (192)

           magical delights: *Maldoror* 60 (191)

           lack of concern: *Maldoror* 60 (192)

P. 53   **nature."**: *Oeuvres complètes* 388

P. 54   **magnificent splendors**: *Maldoror* 60 (191)

           templated in: *Maldoror* 60 (192)

           visage as to: *Maldoror* 60 (192)

           speaks of the: The pursuit curve is currently defined as the interception curve made by an interceptor maintaining continuous fire on a moving airplane from a position to the rear and side, a fairly advanced mathematical problem for a nineteenth-century lycée student.

P. 55   **enjoy the same**: Catachresis is the use of the wrong word for the context.

P. 58   **written in**: The G.L.M. (Guy Lévis Mano) edition of the *Oeuvres complètes* was published in Paris in 1938 and includes facsimiles of the author's corrected pages along with biographical material.

sympathetic: Soupault's essay is reprinted in the Corti edition, 45-66.

P. 59   **seduction**: "Pancalism" is a term Bachelard found in J. M. Baldwin, *Genetic Theory of Reality* (New York, 1915), where it means an activity that transforms all contemplation of the universe into an affirmation of universal beauty. See Gaston Bachelard, *Water and Dreams*, trans. Edith R. Farrell (Dallas, 1983), 198, n. 25.

P. 60   **well articulated**: Franciscus Roels, author of *Handboek der psychologie* (Utrecht, 1934).

P. 61   **Storch**: Alfred Storch, *The Primitive Archaic Forms of Inner Experience and Thought in Schizophrenia*, trans. Clara Willard (New York, 1924) speaks of the relation of muscle and mind.

The gentle Charles-Louis Philippe: *La Mère et l'enfant* (Paris, 1911), 11.

Hate with its: *Maldoror* 2 (124)

P. 62   **and incense; for**: *Maldoror* 2 (124)

phiques sur: Claude Estève, *Etudes philosophiques sur l'expression littéraire* (Paris, 1939), 207.

metacarpus: *Maldoror* 120 (260)

P. 63   **keeps its freedom**: Henri Wallon, *L'enfant turbulent; étude sur les retards et les anomalies de d'eloppement moteur et mental* (Paris, 1925).

right to left: *Maldoror* 11 (135)

P. 65   **use of language**: *Maldoror* 54 (184)

deafness.": *Maldoror* 51 (181)

cured by Cheselden: William Cheselden (1688-1752), whose *Anatomy of the Human Body* was frequently reprinted in the eighteenth century.

I realize that: *Maldoror* 138 (282)

guaranteed "to: *Maldoror* 80 (214)

ful ocean: *Maldoror* 74 (207)

P. 66   **anacoluthons**: The shift from one construction within a sentence to a totally different one.

thought that Paul Valery: *Monsieur Teste*, Trans. Jackson Mathews (Princeton, 1973), 52-53.

P. 67   **cited by Estève**: Edmond Estève, *Leconte de Lisle: L'homme et l'oeuvre* (Paris, n.d.), 23. Both citations from Estève are on the same page.

P. 68   **have to**: Bachelard implies that transference, the redirection of desires and feelings unconsciously retained from childhood toward the psychoanalyst, would as a model for the act of reading provide a sense of interaction with the text. The reader would come to understand himself through an encounter with his own feelings and desires as they are revealed by the text.

P. 71   **This was . . . Lavater:** Johann Caspar Lavater (1741- 1801), Swiss philosopher and theologian, inventor of the system of physiognomy, which consists of determining psychological and moral character from physical appearance and expression, particularly by discovering resemblances to animal types.

even gives: That is, Messrs. Wolf, Hare, Cat, Cock, Magpie, Rat, Deer, Doe, Bull.

Stello, 84. The translation has been altered ("Badger" for "Blaireau").

P. 73   **Kipling:** There is a peculiar irony in this comparison. Wells's narrative was meant to counter what he considered the sentimentality of Kipling's depiction of the relationship between man and animal. Bachelard's preference for Kipling turns the tables, as it were, by disclosing a kind of "scientific" sentimentality in Wells.

would never have: In French, "Il va, frottant ses reins musculeux qu'il bossue."

P. 74   **growl when:** Bachelard gives no hint of his source for this anecdote.

The animals of: In French,

> Sa chevelure blême, en lanières épaisses,
> Crépitait au travers de l'ombre horriblement;
> Et derrière, en un rauque et long bourdonnement
> Se déroulaient, selon la taille et les espèces
> Les bêtes de la terre et du haut firmament.

like this one: In French, "Dans l'onde où les possons déchirent leur reins blancs."

P. 75   **of Chrysaor:** This is a parodic version of the famous line from Jean Racine's *Phèdre*, "Fille de Minos et de Pasiphaé" (Daughter of Minos and Pasiphae), often cited for its allusive and musical qualities. Bachelard's amusing point is that Leconte de Lisle's language, mythological figures, and even his verbal music are totally derivative.

P. 76   **That comes from:** In French:

> Et voici que j'ai vu, par les ombres nocturnes,
> S'amasser en un bloc les oiseaux taciturnes,
> Se fondre étroitement comme s'ils n'étaient qu'un

Bête hideuse ayant la laideur de chacun,
Araignée avec dents et griffes, toute verte
Comme un Dragon du Nil, et d'écume couverte,
Ecume de fureur muette et du plaisir
De souiller pour autrui ce qu'on ne peut saisir.

P. 77 **says, to place**: Albert Thibaudet, *French Literature from 1789 to Our Era* , Trans. Charles L. Markmann (New York, 1967), 283: ". . . a remarkable painter of animals, the Antoine-Louis Barye of French literature." Cf. Edmond Estève, 127: "Leconte de Lisle is one of our great painters of landscapes and also one of our best painters of animals, the Barye or le Frémiet of French poetry."

P. 79 **in vesanias**: Vesania is a generic term for various mental disturbances.

P. 80 **definition proposed**: André Gide, *Le Prométhée Mal Enchaîné:*, *in Romans, Récits et Soties, Oeuvres Lyriques* (Paris, 1958), 305.

P. 81 **stiaries. Someone**: This inspiration for Rimbaud's poem "Voyelles" was first suggested by H. Héraut, "Du Nouveau sur Rimbaud," *Nouvelle Revue Française* 43:602-608.

P. 83 **Balzac**: Honoré de Balzac, "Avant-propos" to *La Comédie Humaine, Oeuvres complètes*, ed. Marcel Bouteron and Henri Longnon (Paris, 1912), 1:xxvi.
Tristan Tzara: Surrealist poet and founder of the Dadaist movement in 1916.

Bachelard's *Lautréamont*
Or, Psychoanalysis without a Patient

JAMES HILLMAN

1. Our Focus

IN 1939, BACHELARD published two shorter pieces on Lautréamont which became part of his book *Lautréamont* (1940). Together with his *Psychoanalysis of Fire* (1938), *Lautréamont* initiates his studies in the poetic imagination. Lautréamont continued to occupy him: in 1946 he published another short article ("Lautréamont, Poet of Muscles and Cries"). This work was integrated into the augmented edition of 1951 and the new edition of 1963.

I shall focus on this small book for these reasons: to discover what Bachelard means by a complex, especially the Lautréamont complex; to understand what he means by a psychoanalysis; and finally to examine the relevance of his kind of psychoanalysis for psychotherapy.

Since my main concern is Bachelard's import for psychotherapy, I shall not concentrate on the issue of what Bachelard says about the poem *Maldoror* and/or about its author, Isidore Ducasse, whose pen name is Lautréamont. I shall not be examining *directly* Bachelard's contributions either to literary criticism or to the psychoanalysis of a particular literary genius. I shall try, too, to stay clear of literary theory in order to remain with my shortsighted focus.

Bachelard's approach implies a radical theory of psychoanalysis: that we can enter into the depths, the motives, the passions of a written soul without personal contact with a him or a her, that we can perhaps better know this person without knowing him or her personally, that there can be, in short, a psychoanalysis without a patient.

Could this approach bear fruit for psychotherapy, which has been conceived, so far, wholly personally in terms of a patient?

2. Freud's and Jung's "Patients"

The notion of a psychoanalysis without a patient begins already in Freud. Both Schreber and Little Hans, although patients, were not *his* patients, yet he analyzed their cases —and Schreber wholly by means of written text. Freud's main step into patientless analysis was his 1910 publication on Leonardo da Vinci, about which he wrote Jung: ". . . a noble spirit, Leonardo da Vinci, has been posing for me—I have been doing a little psychoanalysis of him." "That would be the first [psychoanalytic] step in the realm of biography."[1] Actually, the first step had already been taken in his analysis of Wilhelm Jensen's novel *Gradiva*; but there Freud could check on the analysis with the Danish author, Mr. Jensen himself, at least testing surmises against the story of the "patient." Further studies followed in this line. In fact, it is often unnoticed that not only did Freud illustrate psychoanalytic theory with literary allusions, but that he also developed much of the theory from such nonpatients as literary texts: "The Theme of the Three Caskets," his studies of Michelangelo, *Hamlet*, Dostoevsky, Goethe, the Bible, and the book on jokes.

Jung likewise examined literary and distant sources. His major case study is actually of a written text. *Transformations and Symbols of the Libido*—the work that immediately occasioned the break with Freud—was the psychoanalysis of a text published in French by Flournoy of Geneva, a lost text that was originally the English-language diary of a young American woman, "Frank Miller." Jung never saw her. Later, in the 1930s, Jung analyzed Nietzsche mainly through

1. *The Freud/Jung Letters*, ed. W. Mcguire, trans. R. Manheim and R. F. C. Hull (Princeton, 1974), para. 160, para. 158.

a study of *Thus Spake Zarathustra*. Jung's impressive and pioneering alchemy study uses material from a patient who worked with another analyst and whom Jung never saw during the first eight months.[2] His major essay in transference is, too, an analysis of a text, not a patient.[3]

Now what is going on here? Is the relationship between the psychoanalysis of a text and psychotherapy like one between the pathology lab and the clinical bed? Psychoanalysis examines the tissue of a corpse for benefit of ill patients. On this analogy psychoanalysis is a medical science, while therapy is a healing art. Though the bodies of corpse and patient differ, there is yet a connection: a likeness of underlying structures in each.

This structure is the complex. When Freud and Jung circumscribe the complex in the written work, they take these pathology lab findings to apply to the living persons (Leonardo, Nietzsche), the topic or author of the "corpse" under analysis. Miss Miller is declared by Jung, after scrutiny of her written text, to be prodromally schizophrenic; Leonardo by Freud to be homosexual.

Freud and Jung, however, could not keep their eyes on the complex. They were inhibited in their psychoanalysis of complexes because they were medical men and primarily therapists of people. So they focused on the effects of the complex upon the semi-imagined, semi-biographical persons of Leonardo, Jensen, Nietzsche, Miss Miller. Bachelard invites us to take the distinction even further between the complex and the person who embodies it. He brackets out the patient. Neither the text nor the author of the text is Bachelard's patient. If we call anything in his analyses the patient, it is Imagination, presenting itself phenomenally in the many complexes.

2. C. G. Jung, *Collected Works*, trans. R. F. C. Hull. 20 vols. (Princeton, 1953–) 12 (1944).
3. Jung, *Collected Works* 16.

Although the analogy with the pathology lab places Bachelard's examination of Lautréamont within the domain of science (where his own career originates) rather than within art, nonetheless the imagination of poetic reverie is Bachelard's focus. We therefore have to shift the terms in accordance with this focus. Under his scrutiny the complexes are not so much lesions or problems as emblems. In Bachelard's hand psychoanalysis shifts from an examination of complexes as disorders which separate one from the world, to an appreciation of complexes as emblems of the ways one engages and embraces the world. That is why, again and again Bachelard insists, not suffering but joy is concomitant with the appearance of complexes: for they are not the tools of the Reality Principle, but of the Unreality Principle. Their appearance makes the world anew.

3. Lautréamont

Before continuing with Bachelard, let us return to Lautréamont, the person and the text. Briefly, the Count de Lautréamont was the *nom de plume* of Isidore Ducasse, born April 4, 1846, in Montevideo, only child of French parents who had emigrated from the Pyrenees to Uruguay. Ducasse died in 1870 during the siege of Paris. No one knows how, why, or of what. He was twenty-four years old.

The book *Maldoror* is a long prose poem consisting of six cantos divided into many strophes or stanzas per canto. It did not appear in Ducasse's lifetime, having been held up by the publisher for fear of prosecution for its scandalous contents.

To give you its flavor, here is a representative famous passage: the mating of the hero with a huge mother shark. Maldoror with his knife enters a struggle among sharks, on the side of the huge female shark. This description follows:

> Two sinewy thighs gripped the viscous skin of the monster closely, like two leeches; arms and fins entwined themselves lovingly around

the body of the loved one, as their throats and breasts came to form a single glaucous mass that reeked of seaweed; in the middle of the storm that raged on; in the flashes of lightning, a foamy wave their marriage bed, borne off by a cradling undersea current and rolling over one another into the depths of the abyss, they are united in a coupling that is long, hideous, and chaste.[4]

As Bachelard says, Ducasse eludes the first principle of a biographical study (see 56 above). Ducasse was unknown and then disappeared. No certain likeness of him exists. Although the most assiduous research campaign has been carried out in Uruguay, the south of France, and in Paris since 1939, Bachelard's (56) judgment still holds: a personalistic enlightenment of the work by reference to the author's history is impossible.

The work, however, has been subject to intense and passionate comment by Léon Bloy, Remy de Gourmont, Ruben Dario, André Gide, Huysmans, the Surrealists who regarded it as a sacred text, Malraux, Camus, Henry Miller, Artaud, Aimé Césaire, Maurice Blanchot, as well as lesser-known critics who have devoted entire studies to the poem and to searching out Ducasse through the poem. A man, "Ducasse," in the persona of Lautréamont, has been reconstructed through a variety of analyses of the work.

4. The Lautréamont Complex

But this reconstructed and psychoanalyzed "Ducasse" is not identical with Lautréamont. The reasons for this, in Bachelard's view, are not biographical and historical—there are too few facts about the life of Ducasse. The reason that Lautréamont is not Ducasse is more fundamentally because "a work of genius is the antithesis of life" (58). Or, as he writes later, the fertilizer does not explain the flower.[5] For Bachelard, a poetic image is a source of being, and there is no reality prior

---

4. Isidore Ducasse (Le Compte de Lautréamont), *Oeuvres complètes* (Paris, 1958), 211. Also see above, 25. Subsequent references to Bachelard's *Lautréamont* are noted in the text.

5. Gaston Bachelard, *The Poetics of Space*, trans. Marie Jolas (Boston, 1969), xvi.

to it.[6] Bachelard even claims that the Lautréamont complex derives from the Imagination and not from the imagination of the obscure writer, Ducasse. The name "Lautréamont Complex" signifies for Bachelard a particular style of imagining, one that Ducasse gave voice to.

At the conclusion of his book on fire, Bachelard writes:

> Imagination escapes the determination of psychology—including psychoanalysis—and constitutes a realm that is autochthonous, autogenic. We subscribe to this view: more than the will, more than the élan vital, the Imagination is the very force of psychic production. Psychically, we are created by our reveries. Created and limited by our reverie, for it is reveries that design the final confines of our spirit.[7]

So we cannot truly psychoanalyze the Imagination, if by psychoanalysis is meant a personalistic reduction. But we can do what Bachelard calls a "psychoanalysis" of the reveries, the images, the metaphors in the language that the Imagination speaks. "The Imagination," he says, "speaks in us, our dreams speak, our thoughts speak. Every human activity desires to speak. . . ."[8]

Now for Bachelard, the reveries, images and metaphors that he subjects to his psychoanalysis are not "mental pictures" which are later converted into words. They are originally spoken. A complex shows itself in speech. We see then, first, that the Lautréamont complex is revealed in speech as a *specific* combination of images, metaphors, reveries. That is our first finding. It serves to remind us that Jung also described the complex by examining speech, the disturbances of the word-association, and Freud by examining the speech of dreams, jokes, and slips of the tongue.

Our second finding derives from a negative distinction: the distinction between *complex* and *theme*. Lautréamont and *Maldoror* have been carefully analyzed into themes: rebellion

6. Gaston Bachelard, *L'air et les songes* (Paris, 1943), 283–85.
7. Gaston Bachelard, *The Psychoanalysis of Fire*, trans. Alan C. M. Ross (London, 1964), 110. Translation amended.
8. Bachelard, *L'air et les songes*, 283–85.

against the father; mother-incest; adolescence; dualisms of extreme violence and extreme passivity; the artist-outlaw; the exploration of the perverse and decadent; dualism between God and Devil; evil; homosexuality and masturbation; androgyny; the God Mercury; and also the poetic act. All these thematics may be disclosed by *Maldoror*, and the work may be read in the light of these themes, but for Bachelard themes do not constitute the Imagination. These themes are not specific to, or indicative of, the Lautréamont complex. The same themes may be found in many other works by adolescents, by rebels, by satanists, by sexual extremists. Yet in these works we may not discover the Imagination speaking the Lautréamont complex; indeed, in derivative poetic works, a complex, hence Imagination, might not speak at all, even though the themes persist. A complex is not a theme. Moreover, to seize the work by means of these themes is to negate the poetic images which are new and specific to Lautréamont.

Thematic understanding is always a reduction. No matter how psychiatrically astute or psychologically perceptive, it is not this type of psychoanalysis that Bachelard means. For him, psychoanalysis must stay with the utter originality of the image-complex which cannot be transposed into an already known theme.

Because the Imagination consists in or reveals itself only in distinctly specific image complexes (that may broaden or narrow into themes), we cannot transpose the Lautréamont complex to more majestic *topoi* such as Decadence, or Lucifer, or the Puer Aeternus, without violating the originality of the poetic image.

Originality—that is the third finding that characterizes Bachelard's notion of a complex. He writes in italics: "*Originality is by necessity a complex, and a complex is never very original*" (68). That a complex is "never really original" means to me that the Imagination as such is not really original, because, as archetypal, it is subject to the same ever-recurring, ubiquitous configurations and concerns. The other half of the complex—that "originality is necessarily a complex"—means to me that originality does not altogether depend on the formative abilities of the individual person. For example, when discussing a poor poem by O'Neddy, Bachelard indicates that a good poetic image is not one that is necessarily well written, but is one that is carried by the originality of the complex, in this particular case, the Hoff-mann, complex. "The reader's unconscious makes up for the inadequacy of the poet's unconscious."[9] Imaginative original-ity presents a complex and is given necessarily with any com-plex. Where there is a complex, there is also originality. This has huge implications for our individual complex-ridden psy-chopathology: there is necessarily an originating potential in every complex of the Imagination.

What constitutes the force of a complex, what gives it its dynamism, is the sum of contradictions it amasses in itself. In the case of the Lautréamont complex the supreme contradic-tion is the primitive ambiguity of fear and cruelty, "like lava and ashes . . . from the same crater" (70). Here we must be careful. Fear and cruelty sound like another dualism, another theme. Bachelard, however, derives his thematics not from a dualistic grid that he places on the work, but rather from the particular contradictory images which appear in the Lautré-amont complex. Its images and reveries amass the contra-dictions of fear and cruelty, just as other complexes in the elemental regions of Water and Fire, say, amass other con-tradictions.

Precisely the poetic condensation of these amassed contra-dictions distinguishes the poetic reveries of Lautréamont from look-alikes. Lavater, the Swiss physiognomist, H. G. Wells in his *Island of Dr. Moreau*, Kipling's *Jungle Book*, and the *Poèmes Barbares* of Leconte de Lisle all used similar con-

9. Bachelard, *The Psychoanalysis of Fire*, 89.

tents—the animal in human shape, the animalization of the human—and might be said, on the basis of this theme, to exhibit the Lautréamont complex. Yet these "animalizations," similar in theme, differ in poetic metaphor. Their metaphors fail to distort nature and life into what is beyond nature and life. The similarities of these works to *Maldoror* exist only on a high level of abstraction, a level which misses the precision of form in a complex, according to Bachelard.

Summarizing our findings thus far, we can say: A complex is revealed by precision of content, by originality (e.g., that it has no antecedents), by force of its self-contradictions (the *complexio oppositorum* of Jung), by transformational or deformational novelty (in its images—all of which together imply the complex is not fully susceptible to intellectual understanding). Here we must realize that for Bachelard complexes are "unconscious." They address us beyond our conscious comprehension, as the Hoffmann complex in O'Neddy's poor poem addresses the reader's unconscious. Complex-images speak to us beyond the mind's capacity to understand. This happens because the imagination is not the faculty for forming images of reality; it is the faculty for forming images which go beyond reality, which *sing* reality. It is a superhuman faculty. Man is a man to the extent that he is a superman. A man should be defined by the sum of those tendencies which impel him to surpass the *human condition*.[10]

The Lautréamont complex is a supreme case of this pressing "beyond the human condition." Violence and aggression are central to how the Lautréamont complex pushes beyond the human, and Bachelard devotes two chapters of his small book to violence. But the violence remains held within the poetic images that present it. These images locate the violence in a realm that is prehuman, alien, a world never humanized, never philosophized. Beyond understanding, it

10. Gaston Bachelard, *Water and Dreams*, trans. Edith R. Farrell (Dallas, 1983), 16.

truly bespeaks Bachelard's requirement that imagination, as exhibited in the violence of the Lautréamont complex, presses beyond the human.

How, then, do we recognize, understand, know a complex, if it is superhuman and beyond intellectual grasp? And is this position not a romanticism of feeling or an anti-intellectual primitivism? The answer here is our last finding. Bachelard writes: "I am able to comprehend a soul only in transforming mine, 'as one transforms one's hand by placing it in another's' (Eluard)." "In the life of the passions—our usual life—we can understand ourselves only by *activating* the same complexes" (69).

Activation of the same complex in my own soul, that sympathy for which Bachelard deliberately borrows from psychoanalysis that term "transference," is not the all of it. In the life of *thought*, of analysis, something further is needed. Understanding requires a paradoxical double movement of both transference and diagrammatic reduction of metaphors, like the axial geometry of a flower without which the real flower would not exist.[11] "A complex can be understood only through a course of activation and reduction" (69). Psychotherapy might call this double path empathy and distance at once, or speak of having one foot in and one foot out, or as the Jesuits might say, the truth is not a balance somewhere of two antagonistic ways, but both together, side by side. The complex is grasped only by extreme means, by a consciousness structurally informed and passionately deformed by imagination. This paradox constitutes Bachelardian psychoanalysis.

5. Pathology and Images

Animals are the particular stuff of the Lautréamont complex. They are the *surhumain*, without human meaning, without human feeling, beyond the human condition, a foreign song.

11. Bachelard, *The Psychoanalysis of Fire*, 109.

This animal stuff is disclosed not merely by the 185 animal forms that Bachelard counts in the poem, but also in Maldoror's obscenely terrible and frenetic acts; by the particular body parts and actions of animals: by their talons, teeth, jaws and beaks; by their screams and sucking vampirism; by the expression of a cruel will to pinch, claw, clasp, lacerate, tear with nervous fingers.

These specific qualities of the bestiary show the specific character of the Lautréamont complex: its fundamental animality. In fact, says Bachelard, "a need to animalize . . . is at the origins of the imagination," whose first function "is to create animal forms" (27). The complex expressing itself in the animals creates an active and screaming universe in which fear, brutality, and rage shape imagination, a universe in which "energy is an aesthetic" (66).

This obscure phrase—"in this universe the energy is aesthetic"—closes his chapter on muscles and cries. The phrase refers to the human scream which sounds forth the animality of "an angry universe" (65). "All animals, even those least on the offensive, articulate their war cry" (66). In this sounding, the *dynamis* of nature becomes aesthetic. And if we carry this insight further, all aesthetic reactions of our nostrils, muscles, throat and teeth are the force of nature through us, nature acting upon nature, speaking with nature.

The animalizing tendency begins not in a human need; we do not invent animal symbolisms. Imagination itself invents animal forms, even out there in nature; animals themselves, out there in nature, are living symbols. Primordial brutal life is symbolic, aesthetic—and cruel. ("Cruelty must be placed at the origins of instinct; without it *animal behavior* cannot begin" [85].) The universe when perceived via the Lautréamont complex is aesthetic because it is animal. And it is from the animals that we have learned symbolism. Freudian and literary symbolisms are but mutilated examples of the symbolic powers already in action in nature (31).

As we have seen, for Bachelard, originating powers reside in a complex. So, the poetic reveries of Lautréamont enable us, mere readers in a chair, to recuperate the vital symbolism displayed in these imaginal animals. Instinct returns via these cruel and fearful poetic images. We are restored to the originating symbolism speaking to us as animals as they shriek and rip their way through *Maldoror*. And as they shrieked and ripped their way through the personal imagination of Isidore Ducasse. ("Ducasse's imagination is *natural*" [27].) Ducasse has been judged a paranoid schizophrenic by at least one critic and, by others, a sadist suffering from a kind of violent narcissism. There are many reconstructions of Ducasse as severely pathological. Bachelard circumvents these speculations.

Just as he does not locate the work in pathology, so too he does not locate whatever pathology may be seen in the work to be in the man, Ducasse. Bachelard writes: "We must always return to the work in order to understand the poet. A work of genius is the antithesis of life" (58). Pathology does not originate Imagination, which is originality itself; only a complex originates. With this stroke, Bachelard reverses the whole order of pathologizing. The pathologizing, whether in Ducasse or in the poem, has its source in the images of the Lautréamont complex, in the animals.

It is the animal itself, he says, that is the alienated one and the various animal shapes are various forms of mental alienation (80), just as all our vices are concretized in the animal kingdom (26). So we must locate whatever pathologies we find in these primordial images. Bachelard (79) quotes Jung: "It is almost impossible to escape the power of primordial images." Neither Ducasse nor *Maldoror*, nor we readers, escape. The strangeness in the author, in the text and that we experience in reading derive from the primordial images of the Lautréamont complex in which we, through sympathy, find the *locus classicus* of our own inhuman fears and inhuman cruelties.

Here we notice Bachelard's profound grasp of the human soul's *surhumain* condition as also inhuman, deformed, pathologized. Ducasse's imagination is natural, yes; but not in a Rousseauistic sense of natural. Not things as they are, but as they metaphorize and metamorphozise, for "it is in the study of image distortion that we find the full extent of poetic imagination" (30). "Metamorphosis thus becomes the specific function of the imagination" (88). The appeal to "animal" in both Lautréamont and *Lautréamont* is thus never to the merely natural, whether as pure barbarism or seductive sentimentalism. The appeal is to the animal as natural metaphor.

The contradictions of fear and cruelty and the paradox of empathy and distance sophisticate the merely natural. These double movements and the condensations of metaphors free the person from identification with the literal or nonpoetic demands of emotion. The mix—for instance, of aggression and tenderness (that scene with the shark) or of pity and holocaust—inhibits the *monomania* of instinct, resolving it into multiple and multicolored feelings. For Bachelard, this is the truly human cure of inhuman aberrations (81). Note well that his cure maintains the complex as a full complexity of emotions and images, always capable of metamorphosis, even as the cure detaches the person from the singleness of identification.

Bachelard's psychoanalysis here offers psychotherapy two insights. First, what makes Ducasse exceptional, what takes him beyond himself, beyond the mediocrity of his adolescence, his milieu, and his time is the very complex that also originates that exceptionality considered pathological. The *extremis* of pathology does not yield to the reductive terms of a personalistic or vitalistic psychology. Pathology is rather disclosed by the analysis of poetic images, a metaphorical reduction—itself a *contradictio in adiecto*. As we study Ducasse through Lautréamont, so psychopathology becomes the study of images. Or in the words of Wallace Stevens: "the study of his images Is the study of man. . . . "[12] Second, an empathic understanding of the patient means holding the hand of the complex, slipping one's hand into the patient's images, into his text or what psychotherapists call his "material": dreams, fantasies, reveries. Complexes together, holding hands, yours and mine. Yet not truly "yours" or "mine," but rather an empathetic parallelism of imaginations. And because we are not dealing here with personalistic reductions, imaginations can connect even when distant in place and removed by time, as in the parallel imaginations of reader and writer.

6. Complexes and Imagism: Jung and Pound

I have referred to Jung a few times. Bachelard does too, and rightly so, because Jung invented the term "complex." The term simply means a group of individual ideas held together by a common feeling-tone. "The influence of a complex on thinking and behavior is called a constellation."[13] The Lautréamont complex can be said to be constelled in the life of Ducasse and in the language of *Maldoror*.

What Jung called a complex, Pound called an image. For Pound, an image is "that which presents an intellectual and emotional complex in an instant of time." "The Image is more than an Idea. It is a vortex or cluster of fused ideas and is endowed with energy." An Image is "a Vortex, from which and through which, and into which, ideas are constantly rushing."[14] Jung sought to measure this energetic aspect in his association experiments. From a Bachelardian perspective rushing energy is essential only to certain regions of the Imagination: to fire, for instance, or to the animal fury of the Lautréamont complex, that active, screaming universe.

12. Wallace Stevens, "Study of Images I," in *Collected Poems* (New York, 1978), 463.
13. Jung, *Collected Works* 2: 733.
14. Cited in *Ezra Pound: A Critical Anthology*, ed. J. P. Sullivan (Harmondsworth & Baltimore, 1970), 41, 57.

Rushing instaneity is certainly not constellated by the realms of earthly repose or the dreams of water. Pound's description—to use Jung's language—is itself *complex-bedingt*. All descriptions of complexes are themselves metaphors conditioned by the root metaphors of the complexes themselves. There is no way out: we are never free of Imagination.

In many passages Jung speaks of the complexes as "the little people," "hobgoblins," "revolting vassals in an empire," "small secondary minds," possessing all the characteristics of a separate personality.[15] Complexes are the ground of the belief in spirits and were experienced in antiquity as demons. There is no good reason, he says, for not accepting the complexes as personified from the beginning, subpersonalities as persons *sui generis*.[16] Jung does not quite carry through with this sense of the complex as person. At first he names a complex for its organizing content (e.g. a "pregnancy" complex); later he gives such names as mother, anima, ego, a naming that strikes a compromise with the claims of scientific nomenclature.

That Bachelard calls complexes with personal names—Lautréamont, Empedocles, Novalis, Ophelia, Hoffmann—ties the personified complex more tightly to historical and literary personages. Moreover, the proper names emphasize the originating power of the complex as exemplified in these personifications of poetic reverie. Not that Novalis or Hoffmann invented the complexes which bear their names. Rather, these biographical realities incorporated a genius, a primordial person or demon, which manifests itself in reveries on life and on art, reveries sustained by the life and work of Mr. Novalis and Mr. Hoffmann. The complex is thus the genius, and so the analysis of genius and of a work of genius is a psychoanalysis of a complex, an analysis other than, and maybe even prior to, that of the human person in whom it is con-

15. Jung, *Collected Works* 2: 1352.
16. Jung, *Collected Works* 13: 62, 299.

stellated, the human person who only partly, and sometimes most feebly, embodies the genius. As Jung said, not Goethe created Faust; but Faust, the Faust complex we might say, created Goethe.

Allow me one more phrase from Jung that is so close to Bachelard: "I conceive a complex to be a collection of *imaginings*."[17] These imaginings can be trapped in the grid of the association experiment as a collection of single words. For instance: burn, fire, water, window, smoke, rescue, frightful, red—all of which are held together, says Jung,[18] by the feeling-tone of terror. Compare Lautréamont's beak, jaw, claw, crab, bite, pinch, and shark held together by the emotions of fear and cruelty.

Jung, unlike Bachelard, always stresses the disturbing character of the complex. It crosses your path, it goes against your will, like Socrates' genius who spoke only a "No." More than disturbing, a complex is "painful,"[19] which explains why recognition of complexes in one's life tends to be evaded wherever possible. Jung's work as therapist attends to complexes in those who evade and suffer from that evasion: the lives of neurotics. Bachelard's work as reader attends to where complexes come to flower in the texts of genius. Repression is the focus of one, expression the focus of the other; and so suffering is the emphasis of one, happiness the other. Yet both kinds of psychoanalysis promote a similar therapy: the activation of imaginings. This is because the "Imagination is the true source of psychic production,"[20] and because "the psyche consists essentially of images."[21]

Imaginative activity is not merely a specific remedy for repressed complexes. Rather, this activity allows them their supreme function of organizing the mind around the meta-

17. Jung, *Collected Works* 2: 1352. Italics mine.
18. Jung, *Collected Works* 2: 890–91.
19. Jung, *Collected Works* 2: 1351.
20. Bachelard, *The Psychoanalysis of Fire*, 110.
21. Jung, *Collected Works* 8: 618.

phors of its complexes. These metaphors coordinate, provide a syntax. As well they release the mind into its originality beyond the old entrapped condition, and they invoke the *surhumain*. Is this not cure? Here, Jung and Bachlelard reach back toward Neoplatonic formulations. Poetic metaphors (as told for instance in myths) profoundly coordinate the imaginings of the stray mind. *Mens sana* requires a healthy body of poetic metaphors, else the complexes have no syntax. As Bachelard says: "A poetic mind [and each mind, since it consists essentially of images, is poetic] is purely and simply a syntax of metaphors."[22]

Bachelard's Lautréamont complex (beak, jaw, claw, crab) or Jung's pregnancy complex (stork, bone-bed, flower, red, blood, pierce)[23] would sound and feel differently were it phrased by an imagist or a Haiku writer. This difference is primarily noticed by the listening ear and not by the analytic mind. It is a sense for the images rather than for meaning, for the poetic condensation rather than for the accumulated evidence. The sensuousness of the new presentation of the complex would, in other words, give it a different feel.

7. Psychotherapy

We come back now to our first question: the import of Bachelard's psychoanalysis for psychotherapy. From what we have seen, it is indeed possible to do a psychoanalysis, that is, uncover profoundly organizing, transformational, and disturbing complexes, and to find their personified names—Hoffmann complex, Empedocles complex, Lautréamont complex—all without a patient.

What use has this analysis for therapy? For it to be therapeutic in the usual sense of treatment aiming to relieve suffering through "self-recognition,"[24] the patient must discover

22. Bachelard, *The Psychoanalysis of Fire*, 109.
23. Jung, *Collected Works* 2: 605.
24. Jung, *Collected Works* 2: 1351.

something of himself in the material analyzed. He must become, through this analysis, signified by its significance. He must experience the complex with both a vocative awareness—being spoken to and called by it—and a locative awareness—experiencing the complex as significant for him, even as located in him.

This last, experiencing the complex as significant for him, even as located in him, gives to the reading of Bachelard on imagination such high value for psychotherapy. His double method of reduction and sympathy both delineates a complex and brings it home. In fact, this is what makes the reading of literature necessary training for therapy. In *good* literature the complexes are exposed and carried inside the reader, evoking self-recognition. We cannot discover all the complexes—Novalis, Empedocles, Lautréamont—in ourselves by personal analysis alone. Reading discovers them to us, in us. I use that cursed preposition "in"—but in whom, in what? Where are the complexes located?

Where is the Lautréamont complex? Is it *in* the person of Ducasse? At times Bachelard uses the adjective "ducassien" to describe the complex. Certainly Ducasse was the affective locus of Lautréamont's violence, fear and cruelty; Ducasse wrote the scenes, presented the animals. Yet, in himself, in his person, he may not have embodied or manifested, or *even experienced*, these traits. The actual character witnesses we have, poor as they are, show Ducasse mild, sensitive, taciturn and correct. As Jung says, complexes can be disclosed through the association method that "were not mentioned at all in the history of the case."[25] The Lautréamont complex may have been undisclosed to Ducasse, not phenomenal in his awareness, not mentioned at all until demonstrated in *Maldoror*.

Are the complexes in the text? Is that where we are to locate them? Certainly this is how we find them, but is the

25. Jung, *Collected Works* 2: 1351.

text where they *are?* Bachelard finds violence in the verbs, aggression in the nouns. (Not in adjectives, by the way, for as he says: "the reader would accept an adjective more readily than a substantive. He would allow remorse to be piercing or vulturelike, but for a real, red, purebred vulture—no longer mythological—to drink blood from the heart and feed on the flesh is just too much" [32].) Indeed, the terms of the complex are there in the text, but what affirms that these terms *are* the complex? Other critics might read, have read, the same text and did not find the Lautréamont complex.

Hence the complex must be *in* Gaston Bachelard who says that one can understand a soul only by transforming one's own, a transference, as one transforms one's hand by transferring it into another's. Would there be a Lautréamont complex without Bachelard? Both yes and no—just as there would be no complex of any sort without Jung, since he first "saw" them. But this becomes absurd—and besides, Bachelard did not sign his name Lautréamont. No matter how close Bachelard's hand is inside the hand of the text, inside the hand of Ducasse, the hand of Bachelard remains Bachelard's, so that he can as well transform himself by holding hands with Empedocles and Novalis.

Well then, fourth, is the complex *in* the reader, the reader who enters into the entire complexity of Ducasse, Lautréamont, *Maldoror,* and Bachelard's text called *Lautréamont?* Is the reader the locus? And what if the reader be old, female, and indolently vegetative, able to bring to hand, to mind, or even to reverie neither fears nor cruel wishes of sharks and knives, betrayals and sperm, claws, cries and tigers? Is the Lautréamont complex in *any* reader at all? As Bachelard says not everything is available to everyone: "the person who listens to the sound of the stream can scarcely comprehend the person who hears the song of the flames: they do not speak the same language."[26] No, the complex is only *in* that

26. Bachelard, *The Psychoanalysis of Fire,* 89.

reader, and *when* that reader, is relocated by self-recognition to *in*clude the complex, that is to say, only when the complex in the act of reading has been troped, displaced by the analysis itself into therapy.

And where was it before it was displaced? Why, "in" the Imagination! And only this place, if such it is, allows the complex to permeate throughout and not be fixed literally in the four others: writer, text, critic, reader, and makes each of them patients, that is, signified and disturbed by the complex. I say "disturbed" because I come from Jung. Bachelard would say "raised," because Imagination is a more-than-human faculty. The raising, however, can go by the way of the disturbing, since the poetic image which reveals the complex is always a decomposition, a deformation, even a destruction, and underlying it are those amassed contradictions, that tearing tension which furnishes the complex its force.

We can conclude then that it is indeed possible to do therapy without a patient, but only when the talk, the reading or considering, brings that moment of locating awareness—not subjectivism, not this is *my* complex ("in" is not a synonym for "my"), not narcissistic identification with that other hand into which you have slipped and so immobilized your own. Rather, this locating awareness that this complex under consideration, for instance, Lautréamont with its adolescent blasphemy, sexual extremities, this complex locates itself in my condition, and I can be found, and found out, in its immediate proximity. *Lautréamont, c'est près de, presque, moi.* The key term for this sense of therapy is not dosage, the art of amounts, but locus, the art of placing and place—and displacing.

Of course, everything I have said, that Bachelard has said, depends utterly on the all-encompassing sense of Imagination as the place in which everything we are saying takes place. If a complex is "in" the Imagination and, if the complexes appearing in reveries, images and metaphors insure as under-writers the shape and limits of the human spirit,[27] then the task of self-recognition, which is the primary task of therapy, means a locational awareness of Imagination by means of the royal road of the complexes. This road opens in the two chairs of the consulting room with a therapist; it opens as well in the single chair, alone with a book.

27. Bachelard, The Psychoanalysis of Fire, 110.
28. For further studies of Bachelard and Lautréamont, see the following: Wallace Fowlie, Lautréamont (New York, 1973); Alex de Jonge, Nightmare Culture (London, 1973); Klaus Winckelmann, Lautréamont Impersonator: A Study in Poetic Autobiography (Ottowa, 1974); Joachim Kopper, "Wissenschaftlicher und poetischer Geist," Anhang to Die Philosophie des Nein (Weisbaden, 1978); Jean-Claude Margolin, Bachelard (Paris, 1974); Francois Dagognet, Gaston Bachelard—sa vie, son oeuvre, avec un exposé de sa philosophie (Paris, 1965); Bachelard-Epistemologie, Textes choisis par Dominique Lecourt, 3rd ed. (Paris, 1980); Edward Casey, "Getting Placed: Soul in Space," Spring 1982 (Dallas, 1982), 1–25.

Bachelard as Literary Critic

ROBERT S. DUPREE

THE LATE THIRTIES, when Bachelard's first works on the imagination took shape, were years that had already begun to loom ominously with emerging forms of power and terror greater than the world had ever known. In turning back to reexamine his *Lautréamont*, one is tempted to see in it a reflection of the fascination with violence that characterized the avant-garde enthusiasms of early modernists like Marinetti or Pound and that led, in some cases, to fascist sympathies. Published virtually on the eve of World War II, Bachelard's book appeared when a Nazi-inspired "aesthetics of violence" was threatening all of Europe. But leftists have never accused Bachelard, as they have Jung, of being a mystical reactionary. He has earned the attention of Marxists like Dominique Lecourt, and no one would accuse him seriously of fascistic tendencies—his withdrawal from academic duties during the war certainly speaks for itself. And though his little book seems to ignore the political implications of a poem that speaks of violence on every page, this omission is not an accident. The sociopolitical implications of *Maldoror* are not completely neglected; rather, in characteristic fashion they are subsumed under a study of "culture complexes." Bachelard refuses to be distracted from his main purpose by any short-range considerations; his intention is to offer a more important lesson about the psychological and aesthetic dimensions of aggression. Yet because of the risk he took in writing it, *Lautréamont* is perhaps Bachelard's most daring book. Not so dazzling a performance as his series on the elements or later books of "poetics," it reveals him nevertheless as a critic willing to venture beyond the limitations of *The Psychoanalysis of Fire* in order to broaden the narrow perspectives of conventional criticism. Indeed, Bachelard's book has been called "a model of analysis" by Pierre-Olivier Walzer,[1] a recent editor of Lautréamont who recognizes the exemplary status of its achievement. But before speaking of Bachelard as literary critic, I must say something about Isidore Ducasse and his own strange achievement.

The author of *Maldoror* died quite young, having published one remarkable book in 1869 and begun another shortly afterward. He was virtually ignored for the next fifteen years until his book was rediscovered by a group of Belgian writers who in turn introduced it to members of the symbolist school in France. But only with its adoption as something of a sacred text by the surrealists in the 1920s did it come to be recognized as a work of major importance, though to be sure the groundwork for this recognition had been laid by many of the critics Bachelard cites (and criticizes) in the course of his analysis.

Maldoror is very much a book of the nineteenth century, despite its greater appeal to twentieth-century readers. It reflects faithfully the new-found fascination with violence that began in the French revolution and was canonized in the biology of Darwin. Like Baudelaire, whom Ducasse recognized as a precursor, Lautréamont builds his poetry out of the grotesque elements of modern urban existence. What Walter Benjamin has to say about *The Flowers of Evil*, in an essay exactly contemporary with Bachelard's *Lautréamont*, applies equally to both poets: "Fear, revulsion, and horror were the emotions which the big-city crowd aroused in those who first observed it. . . . Moving through this traffic involves the individual in a series of shocks and collisions. At dangerous intersections, nervous impulses flow through him in rapid succession, like the energy from a battery."[2]

1. Pierre-Olivier Walzer, "Introduction: D'Isidore Ducasse au Comte de Lautréamont," in Lautréamont, Germain Nouveau, *Oeuvres complètes* (Paris, 1980), 32.
2. Walter Benjamin, "On Some Motifs in Baudelaire," in *Illuminations*, ed. Hannah Arendt (New York, 1969), 174–75.

Ducasse was a native of Montevideo, Uruguay—like Jules Supervielle after him—and must have witnessed the violence of revolution there at an early age. Though certain passages in his poem reflect this past, the immediate inspiration he claimed in letters to his publisher was purely literary and predominately romantic. The various "Satanic schools" that were his acknowledged models are certainly relevant to the mode of *Maldoror*, but Lautréamont goes so far beyond them that they are an insufficient explanation for his unprecedented emphasis on violence. Bachelard, "the philosopher of surrealism,"[3] implies that not even his surrealist followers have managed to capture the dizzy variety of his aggressive energy. Yet *Maldoror* is more akin in some ways to the earlier Futurist movement, with its slogan "Art can only be violence, cruelty, injustice," than to surrealism. The Futurists' emphasis on "the temporal succession of events as perceived in visual art," a "will to destroy all moral codes," and the "phenomena of accelerated sensory change," as Max Kozloff describes certain key features,[4] recalls Bachelard's analysis of the giddiness and speed of Maldoror's metamorphoses and will-to-attack. A "spiritual freedom and a primitive innocence which they opposed to any merely 'aesthetic' purifying of visual means" characterize both the Futurists and their precursor of a half-century earlier. In their rejection of traditional metaphors and all images that merely *reproduce* reality, they make even the Cubists seem pictorial and static by comparison. This kinship runs deep. The preeminence of animal life in *Maldoror* should not blind us to his fascination with the mechanical; the famous encounter of the umbrella and sewing machine on the dissecting table is certainly worthy of Futurism. Furthermore, unlike Cubism, Futurism was as much a literary as an art movement, and its "statements

3. G. C. Christofides, "Bachelard's aesthetics," *Journal of Aesthetics and Art Criticism* 20:263.
4. Max Kozloff, *Cubism/Futurism* (New York, 1974), 119.

generally stressed polymorphous appearances, synesthesia, and the interchangeability of materials and perceptions"[5] with a demonic energy that is pure Lautréamontism. This environment of constant change and ceaseless challenge that had its origins in the nineteenth-century urban environment —whether in Paris or Montevideo—and was given quasi-metaphysical status by natural selection and dialectical materialism became the characteristic landscape of the twentieth century.

"For Lautréamont," says Bachelard, "the Word is violence, Genesis is Gehenna, creation brutality." In this single sentence, he puts his finger on the most striking feature of Ducasse's work, for there is a secular gnosticism in *Maldoror* that would turn all embodiment into evil and disgust. Ducasse's statement to his publisher that driving the imagination so far into evil has a cathartic, moral effect, may have been an attempt to allay fears of prosecution by the authorities, but it is also doctrinally orthodox gnosticism.

> First of all let me explain my situation. I have sung of evil like Mickiewickz, Byron, Milton, Southey, A. de Musset, Baudelaire, and so on. Naturally, I have exaggerated the pitch a little so as to do something new in the context of that sublime literature which sings of despair only to depress the reader and make him long for the good as its remedy. And so it is, in short, always of the good that one sings, except for using a more philosophic and less naïve method than the old school, of which Victor Hugo and several others are the only representatives still living.[6]

While it may seem odd to connect the violent and shocking poetry of Lautréamont with an ancient religious heresy of which he was probably ignorant, there is an obvious parallel between them that helps make sense of the anti-creative aggression and violent action of *Maldoror*. For as Hans Jonas remarks, speaking of "gnostic libertinism:"

5. Kozloff, 121.
6. Ducasse to Verboeckhoven, in Walzer, 296-297.

Beyond the motive of defiance, we find sometimes the freedom to do everything turned into a positive *obligation* to perform every kind of action, with the idea of rendering to nature its own and thereby exhausting its powers. . . . The idea that in sinning something like a program has to be completed, a due rendered as the price of ultimate freedom, is the strongest doctrinal reinforcement of the libertinistic tendency inherent in the gnostic rebellion as such and turns it into a positive prescription of immoralism.[7]

In that way the passages depicting the drunkenness and the conquest of the Creator are a coherent part, not only of the theme of revolt which is present everywhere in the cantos, but also in terms of an evil principle of matter that enchains the free spirit in the flesh. Bachelard, who does not mention gnosticism, nevertheless sees in Lautréamont an important transformation of its main themes. Speaking of Maldoror's copulation with a shark, he asks,

Is consummated love a fall during a moment of forgetfulness? Must we go abruptly from Plato to Chamfort, from platonic love (the encounter of two illusions) to physical love (the encounter of two epiderms)? The epithalamion of the female shark is really a *requiem*. It intones the death of innocence, the disappointment of a pure and juvenile enthusiasm. (26)

The passage is, indeed, both a striking psychological description of an early event in adolescence and, at the same time, an account of the gnostic fall of pure spirit into matter. It combines libertinism and asceticism, those seemingly contradictory but actually complementary components of gnosticism of which Jonas speaks. There is no surprise, then, in Ducasse's reversal in the "Preface to a Future Book" and his declaration that henceforth he will react against his times by reasserting morality and even a kind of asceticism (which is, however, denied by his rich, encyclopedic, and almost comic accumulation of examples and images of the things he rejects). He says in *Poésies II*, "I do not accept evil. Man is

7. Hans Jonas, *The Gnostic Religion* (Boston, 1963), 273-74. Also consult Eric Voegelin, *Science, Politics and Gnosticism* (Chicago, 1968).

perfect. The soul does not fall. Progress exists. The good is irreducible. Antichrists, accusing angels, eternal punishment, religions are the product of doubt." And he adds, "Love of a woman is incompatible with love of humanity. Imperfection must be rejected."[8] Having entered this ascetic stage, Ducasse can claim "I know no other grace than that of having been born. An impartial mind finds it to be complete" (279). The constant attacks against romanticism in the *Poésies* do not contradict this gnostic asceticism, which is evident in such statements as "Lamartine believed that the fall of an angel would become the Elevation of a Man. He was wrong to believe it" (280). Likewise, "In order to describe heaven, one must not bring the materials of earth. Earth and its materials must be left where they are in order to embellish life with its ideal" (285).

Thus Bachelard is correct to see the same mind behind the "Preface," the *Poésies*, and *Maldoror*. They belong to the same stance. Yet there is much that Bachelard finds of more direct interest in Ducasse, such as the statements in the *Poésies* about science, philosophy, and poetry: "I had spent much time in the study of the abstract sciences. The few people with whom one communicates were not such as to make it distasteful for me. When I began the study of man, I saw that these sciences are proper to him, that I went less beyond my condition in penetrating further into them than did others who knew nothing of them. I pardoned them for not taking the trouble! I did not think I would find many companions in studying man. That is the proper study of mankind. I was wrong. There are more who study man than who study geometry" (282). "There exists a logic for poetry. It is not the same as in philosophy. The philosophers are nothing but poets. The poets have the right to consider themselves above philosophers" (286). "The science that I undertake is the distinct science of poetry. I do not sing the latter; I am trying

8. Walzer, 275–76. Subsequent citations are identified in the text.

to find its source" (286). These half-mocking aphorisms suggest that Ducasse was not only a descendant of the gnostics but also a forerunner, in his study of both science and poetry, of Bachelard himself.

Bachelard is no gnostic, but he recognizes clearly, if not overtly, the gnostic temper of his author:

> In fact there seem to be the traces of two different conceptions of the Almighty in Ducasse. There is the Almighty who is the creator of life. It is against this creator of life that Ducasse's violence revolts. There is the Almighty who is the creator of thought. Lautréamont places him in the same cult as he places geometry. (53)

The opposing Gods of gnostic theology, adapted to the post-Cartesian secular mind, could not be more postively identified.

The slim book on the Count of Lautréamont that Gaston Bachelard published in 1939 was even briefer than the more recent "augmented" edition (1983) on which this translation is based. Chapter five, "Lautréamont, Poet of Muscles and Cries," was first published in 1940 and added to the volume later. Nevertheless, the book has a clear unity of design that belies one's first impression of a patchwork collection of separate essays. Its six chapters and conclusion amount to a kind of manifesto for modern poetry, following the first two surrealist manifestoes of André Breton and preceding the third by a few years. Yet, while the central characteristics of the new poetry are shrewdly and carefully spelled out in each of the chapters, where Bachelard insists on the primacy of will, action, creation, and revolt in modern literature and sees in Lautréamont a crucial predecessor of the surrealist enterprise (Breton wrote that "the greatest responsibility for the current state of things poetic falls to this man," and André Gide called him, even more than Rimbaud, "the master of tomorrow's literature"), the main significance of this book is that it provides a coherent and extended critical perspective for the new poetry that the surrealists could not manage. However, what Bachelard offers is not surrealist doctrine but a *vade mecum* for reading all modern poetry. The significance of *Lautréamont* lies less in what Bachelard says about the strange poem that is his subject than in the method he offers for coming to terms with a work of the imagination. Writing some twenty-five or more years after the first appearances of Futurism, Bachelard assumes that modern movements in art and poetry have already had their irreversible impact on the present. In the conclusion to this book, he suggests that it is time to go beyond them. But though he demonstrates that as precursor of the aggressive energy and metamorphic violence of contemporary art Lautréamont can no longer be ignored, he also shows that contemporary criticism is ill-equipped to deal with a text that, while still freshly radical, is nevertheless more than seventy years old. Twentieth-century critics still tend to write as though they were of the same generation as Victor Hugo.

Though Bachelard does no close reading, no exhaustive textual analysis, he is nevertheless what I would call a practical critic in this work. He illustrates with directness and conviction what a literary critic ought to do and what so many modern critics before him failed to do, hence his frequent comments about the shortcomings of current literary criticism. If Bachelard had been more narrowly methodical and academic, he might have produced a French equivalent for the syllabus of interpretive errors set forth by I. A. Richards in *Practical Criticism*, which offers instance after instance of misreading by the educated. But instead of exposing the "stock responses" of *l'homme moyen intellectuel* by having him evaluate and analyze a group of poems whose authors' names have been erased, Bachelard chooses a single poet and a single poem to act as touchstone for his *sottisier*. Without the crutch of the author's name, Richards's participants were forced to fall back on their own taste—that is, their own prejudices—to judge the "anonymous" poems placed before them. Likewise, Bachelard chooses an author about whom almost nothing is known; there is no biography to guide the reader toward some conventional bias for judging the extraordinary language and imagery of *Maldoror*. The critic must look at the poetry itself and judge it for what it is.

It is amusing that Bachelard, the historian and theorist of scientific method, felt no need to set up a "laboratory," as Richards did, of volunteer readers. His approach is phenomenological in that he knows himself well enough to trust his own perceptions. Richards' "scientific" claims for his experiment in reading are belied by his own exquisite taste, which guides him in his selection of protocols as surely as Bachelard's guides his reading of *Maldoror*. Richards contributed little to psychological theory or to a literary psychology because, in fact, the influence of *Practical Criticism* came not from its psychological framework but from its amusing—if embarrassing—exempla. Bachelard's use of "psychoanalysis," by way of contrast, is a loose and imaginative application that has no pretensions whatever to being rigorous or scientific. He psychoanalyzes Ducasse in the same way that he psychoanalyzes fire—not as a person but as a "culture complex." He studies not the author's unconscious but those generalized social forms that have affected every French lycée student in modern times: the bullying rhetoric teacher, the haircut, the rivalry among schoolmates. Bachelard articulates the unconscious rules that force an individual to abide by the imposed conventions of his society. His is not the psychocriticism later developed by Charles Mauron but the method, refined and more disciplined, announced in his previous book. In *Lautréamont* as in *The Psychoanalysis of Fire*, the object of analysis is really a body of cultural assumptions and common experiences which, more than the author's biography, are the basis of his imaginary universe. If Ducasse underwent the indignities of schoolboy persecution, it was as the representative of a certain class of experience, not as the isolated victim of a personal pathology, that he gives his experiences play in his writings. Bachelard insists on the banality of Ducasse's life, its middle-class ordinariness. If anything is psychoanalyzed, it is the world that set the stage for his amazing pyrotechniques in language. Here Bachelard lays the foundation for the work of a later disciple, Michel Foucault.

What is striking about Bachelard's approach is his ability to go right to the heart of the work, refusing to be misled by guidelines of the sort that are usually successful for dealing with more conventional works. First of all, Bachelard approaches *Lautréamont*, in all its seeming perversion and violence, with a spirit neither of detachment nor pretended sympathy but of full-hearted participation. He gives himself completely to the work, accepts its conventions and its world as they are depicted, and deals with *Maldoror* by seeking to discover its center, its main rhythm and insight into the truth of human action. Thus his brief study is a succession of chapters that peel away and open to view, layer by layer, the kernel of Ducasse's strange poem. But in the process of accounting for the imaginative core of the book, Bachelard also evolves a critical method that underpins and helps to demonstrate the spirit of all his commentaries on literary texts.

Thus certain aspects do not interest Bachelard. He is very little concerned with the attention to detail in *Maldoror* or with the often adolescent sensationalism of Ducasse's descriptions. What concerns him, rather, is the "overwhelming energy with which things meet in time throughout *Maldoror*." This language is indicative of a series of abstractions that Bachelard makes from the text in the interest of establishing a kind of poetics of the life force. Indeed, he sees the heart of poetry—or at least of this kind of poetry—as residing less in form than in vortex, less in the reconciliation of opposites than in a constant dialectic of contending forces. "Metaphor" is too weak a word to use for the technique of

Maldoror, and Bachelard, who uses the term "image" so frequently elsewhere, shows relatively little interest in applying it here. Nor does he employ such familiar concepts as "symbol" or "analogy," though they are the vocabulary of many a book he cites approvingly in the course of his ruminations on the elements and on space and time.

Bachelard's purpose in this book is to forge new critical tools appropriate for dealing with a new literature, but his occasionally programmatic tone should not mislead us. What Bachelard is teaching in this little book is nothing less than a revolutionary new way of reading a literary text—an important contribution to the revolution that had already begun, under a different guise, in Anglo-American criticism. For as striking and original as Bachelard's meditations are, they are closely tied to certain fundamental stances that are part and parcel of the development of modern literary theory and criticism, not only in France but in England and America as well.

By selecting a writer whose personal life is as obscure as is Ducasse's, Bachelard deliberately foregoes any conclusions that might be drawn from the author's life. This rejection of the biographical method, which was to characterize the "new criticism" in both America and France, is meant to make a reader confront the work itself and examine *its* meaning, rather than fantasize about the author. Since so very little is known about Ducasse, the temptation is great indeed. Bachelard's choice of his subject may well have been deliberate, even methodological, and his survey of the various prefaces to *Maldoror* reveals the almost comic inconsistencies and false assumptions that emerge from the pens of some of the most respected of literary critics.

Bachelard argues against the same twins of intentional and affective fallacies later dissected by W. K. Wimsatt and Monroe Beardsley. For *Maldoror* is a book that, almost more than any other, resists being read literally; yet, as Bachelard recognizes, here lies the greatest temptation of all. Critics are embarrassingly prone to mistake poetic violence for a recommendation of or invitation to physical violence. In his chapter on "Human Violence and Culture Complexes," Bachelard pauses in his examination of Maldoror's revolt against God to issue a caveat:

> Thus the lines of this axis reveal a Lautréamontism raised almost inevitably to a blasphemous pitch. But here I must emphasize that this life-driven inflation is the result of literary expression. In short, Isidore Ducasse's life was peaceful. Nothing in it recalls the actual revolt carried out by a Rimbaud. . . . It is a drama of education, born in a writing class, a drama which must be resolved in a work of literature. (41)

Though Ducasse's need to "pronounce his violence" may have had its origins in the schoolroom and as a revolt against the tyranny of his writing instructor, his school years were altogether typical ones. The poetry of *Maldoror* resides in its violent *use* of language through what Bachelard calls an "astonishing unity" of disparate things that are brought together in surprising and unusual ways. *Maldoror* is not a symptom of something in its author but a dramatic presentation of something in man, in his human nature, which can only be expressed in terms of animal violence or revolt or extreme consciousness of suffering, inflicted or undergone. It is a fable that is closer to existentialism in its view of man than to surrealism, under whose banner it was revived and extolled. But Bachelard rightly recognizes that the shock value of *Maldoror* is meant to educate the imagination. "Lautréamont does not care to seduce; he wants to carry away his prey in a single stroke. He is insidious only in order to upset the reader's systematically sluggish, non-dynamized imagination" (44).

Bachelard sees Lautréamont as the antidote to a static, purely visual imagination: "Ducasse's poetry must not be analyzed in terms of visual images but of kinetic ones. The poetry must be judged as an especially abundant system of reflexes, not as a collection of impressions" (44). Bachelard emphasizes, as does the Russian critic Mikhail Bakhtin, the presence of "innumerable *bodily images*, accelerated active projections." For Lautréamont *produces* rather than *reproduces* images; his fertile imagination creates new beings and shows them as the temporal conjunction of two actions. The object of Ducasse's art is to reawaken the imagination by an appeal to the dormant energies within our bodies by forcing the will to participate in the imaginative realm. Critics who speak of Ducasse's "madness" are dismissed with a shake of the head as intelligent readers who ought to know better:

> We can see that literary critics have no notion of the complexity of madness. An even stranger ignorance is evident in the way that they fail to penetrate the significance of a notion indispensable for understanding the basic psychological function of literature—that is, the notion of *madness written down*. (46)

Bachelard goes on to speak of "sublimation," not in the way it "is misused in current psychoanalytic criticism" but as "a true objective crystallization. Man is crystalized in the peculiar system of the book. Never has a progressive crystalization been so clear, perhaps, as in Lautréamont's case" (47). By speaking of "literary sublimation," then, Bachelard means to emphasize that *Maldoror* is, after all, not a personal confession, a case history, or a collection of symptoms but a work of art. Bachelard defends the unity of the work, "its resonant coherence," by insisting on the control exercised by the author: "In its very aberration it is not aberrant. It is a madness lacking in insanity" (47). What, then, is *Maldoror* about? It is about the interchange between reader and text. "I can understand another soul only by transforming my own" (69). "The poet must create his reader," Bachelard proclaims at the beginning of chapter five.

In the course of getting to the heart of Lautréamont, Bachelard compares him with not only with Rimbaud and

Baudelaire, but also with La Fontaine, Hugo, Huysmans, Leconte de Lisle, Kafka, Casanova, Sade, Dostoevsky, H. G. Wells, Kipling, Nietzsche, and Mayakovsky. He criticizes in Wells "the large number of adjectives" and the attempt to cover up a failure of imagination with pseudo-scientific pretensions. The irony of Wells's *The Island of Dr. Moreau*, which was intended in part as a satiric attack on what he considered the sentimentality of Kipling's *Jungle Book*, is that the parody, in Bachelard's view, is less convincing than the original. Kipling's depiction of animality is truer and more believable than Wells's. For Bachelard is no uncritical ad-mirer of the poets he assembles in such abundance to illus-trate his points. He admits to finding in Leconte de Lisle a poet of some charm, yet he also shows just how limited and conventional that charm is. La Fontaine is compared with Lautréamont not so that a great poet of French classicism will appear to disadvantage but so that the manner of *Maldoror* will not be confused with the conventions of the animal fable. Of course as one of the poets of the Grande Epoque, La Fontaine is an almost obligatory foil for the new classic of the age of surrealism. Bachelard is intent on making his readers see that literature has entered a new era, one that must take account of the nightmare world of Flaubert's Saint Anthony or of Kafka's cockroach. Critics who praise Le-conte de Lisle for the vividness of his animal portraits or Wells for his knowledge of science are put to shame for their extravagance and ignorance. Ducasse, who knew enough mathematics to understand a pursuit curve, commands a bestiary and a knowledge of zoological detail that makes their depictions of animality seem as naïve and toy-like a world as La Fontaine's. While Bachelard would certainly defend La Fontaine on his own terms and does not wish to dismiss Leconte de Lisle completely, he insists that critics have no ex-cuse for finding great powers of animal imagination in third-rate works like *The Island of Dr. Moreau* or *Toilers of the Sea*.

Far from being averse to making critical judgments, Bachelard assesses his examples, compares and contrasts the successes and the failures, and makes careful distinctions between the genius of a Kafka—whose metamorphic imagination retards reality—and a Lautréamont—whose imagination accelerates and violates reality.

Bachelard sees in Lautréamont a refusal of mere mimesis; he says that animal forms "are more *produced* than reproduced" in *Maldoror*, thus anticipating the antimimeticism of so much recent philosophical and literary theory. Lautréamont evokes no presences; his poetry is given over totally to the fact of change, to metamorphosis, to the human will that makes connections between things as "liaisons temporelles," as objects meeting one another for a moment in time. This conjunction of disparate things suggests that the world is made up of momentary metaphors. Like Fernand de Saussure's arbitrarily conjoined signifier and signified, Lautréamont's reality is constructed out of difference. Such a view of the world rejects, as Bachelard recognizes, any notion of nature as something to be mirrored in art. Lautréamont's interest in natural history, as reported by a former schoolmate, explains nothing, since *Maldoror* does not imitate or depict anything real. He never lingers before an object. Rather, he discloses some transforming energy that underlies all things and that is not specifically human. In this Lautréamont (and Bachelard) anticipates the current trends exhibited in the thought of Jacques Derrida or Richard Rorty. Bachelard, reading Ducasse, becomes the first deconstructionist, but he acknowledges in others—in Armand Petitjean, for instance—a recognition of the "*res novae* within and without us," where "the value of clarity activates the imagination and moves it from imitation to creation. . . . The imagination will no longer be merely equal to whatever has already happened in the past" (87). In the end, Bachelard insists on what Petitjean calls "the mutual obligation between object and subject" which abolishes mere chance (88). What Bachelard offers us, almost half a century after his book was published, is an alternative to much of the scepticism that constitutes our present transitional postmodernism in literary theory, for he already understands what we are just beginning to see: that the mind must be free for the "metaphor of metaphor," for "a joy of abstracting, a joy of being man" (90). It is not in the imitation of action but "in the *dream of action* that the truly human joy of action resides" (90). The question for Bachelard is how to "bring about truly human, anagenetic, *open* metamorphoses" (90), how to produce rather than merely reproduce reality. For him, the answer lies in recognizing that "life must desire thought" and that "a specifically human value is always a *converted* natural value" (91). Lautréamont always speaks in the present tense; his is a synchronic imagination that has no diachronic dimensions, like de Saussure's approach to language. Lautréamont's images are not mere reflections of an external reality, much less realistic descriptions of human behavior. They are an attempt to break with traditional modes of representation, such as those described by E. H. Gombrich in his familiar study *Art and Illusion*. Our images of animals are permeated with the representational categories that Bachelard describes as ready-made. Thus he has already anticipated what art historians were to discover only decades later.

But by far the most important point that Bachelard has to make in this book concerns literalism. Only an exceptionally naïve critic could take *Maldoror* literally, though such readers are perhaps more numerous than one would suppose. Bachelard chooses his author and text to show that the essential quality of a truly imaginative work is its resistance to literalization, that is, mere reduction to or reproduction of an uncritically perceived reality. The acts described in Ducasse's poem are so outrageous that they cannot possibly be taken as literal accounts of human behavior. They must be understood not as physical but as verbal violence. The metaphor is a form of verbal violence, but in Lautréamont the metaphors—if that is what these temporal connections between accelerating entities should be called—are a moving target. Like Dante, like Milton, and like Baudelaire, Ducasse had to create a new kind of reader, one who could grasp that reading such a work requires a different kind of commitment —the duty to interpret, to participate, to become one with its images of energy. Dante, Milton, and Baudelaire, like Lautréamont, force us to recognize that we are their hypocritical brothers, their doubles, as fallen and violent as the actors in their imaginary dramas.

The center of literalism, however, remains the biographical fallacy. Bachelard insists repeatedly that internal evidence alone is sufficient and alone reliable for making judgments about the author; Ducasse's mathematical abilities, for instance, cannot be demonstrated from what we know of his life, but they are convincingly displayed in his book. At the same time as the Anglo-American "new critics" were warning against the biographical fallacy in the English-speaking world, Bachelard was offering—independently and virtually alone—a massive demonstration of its dangers. Likewise, he defends the essential unity of *Maldoror* and refuses to read Lautréamont's strange book as anything but a work of art, complete and whole on its own aesthetic terms: "Contemplating a profound work leads us to ask psychological questions which a detailed biographical examination could never answer. There are minds for which *expression* is more than life and other than life" (55). Though these remarks are certainly different from any made by the American critics, they are very much in the same spirit. It is the work that one studies, not the life of the author. Literalism and biographism go hand in hand; they bring us not closer to Ducasse's purpose but further from it.

For Lautréamont's Cartesian violence is too calculating and rational to be the product of a deranged mind. It is a purely verbal violence that speaks not of physical acts but of the inner violence of reason as an instrument of tyranny and constraint, like Blake's "mind-forg'd manacles." Thus Ducasse's curious admiration of both violence and mathematics expresses a consistency of mind, not a contradiction or a state of psychosis. The violence imagined in the narrative is neither an imitation of nor an incitement to physical violence. It is the logical conclusion of a line of reasoning; like Dostoevsky's Raskolnikov, Lautréamont sees violence as the necessary outcome of certain systematic principles put into practice.

In speaking of education and bullying, Bachelard situates these systematic principles at the heart of the educational enterprise, anticipating the hidden roots of social power and control later elaborated by Ivan Illich and Michel Foucault. Bachelard ties French rationalism and violence together neatly as complementary aspects of cultural expression, systematically inculcated by the school. Lautréamont may indeed seem schoolboyish in the extremes to which he carries his parodic gestures, but Bachelard makes this adolescent posturing assume a dual significance. The very puerility of the revolt points to a radical stage of consciousness forced upon the child by his society and its institutions. Bachelard draws on the tyrannies of the lycée—tyrannies common to most nineteenth-century schools—to show how a kind of Darwinian survivalism emerges from a repressive milieu and issues forth in the extremes characteristic of the rebel Maldoror. The adolescent hero, so prominent in the twentieth century, is born and further shaped by the banal power struggles inherent in Tom Brown's schooldays. He is the prescient figure of the antihero who has become common a century later in an age of even greater and more widespread anxiety.

The aesthetic side of violence, explored in Futurism and Vorticism, is thus continuous with the same historical experience that makes up Bachelard's cultural or educational "complex." Ezra Pound, for instance, spoke of the way that "an organisation of forms expresses a confluence of forces" and wrote of the "new and swift perceptions of forms" that were emerging. He noted the "beauty of machines in those parts of the machine where the energy is most concentrated. Probably maximum at these points, 'points of crisis.'" "All experience rushes into this vortex." Pound's interest in violence and energy is part of the same revolt against the nineteenth-century rhetoric teacher. He says that "machines are in a 'healthy state' because one can still think about the machine without dragging in the private life and personality of the inventor." Thus "the vorticist relies not upon similarity or analogy, not upon likeness or mimicry. . . . VORTICISM is art before it has spread itself into a state of flaccidity, of elaboration, of secondary applications." Bachelard acknowledges both sides of violence, analyzes its sources, and sees its verbal production and presentation not as mere manifestations of revolt, assignable to certain social causes, but as assertions of vitality and life; for like Pound, Bachelard had a quarrel with Bergson's tidy vision of the *élan vital* and preferred to invest his own energies in tirelessly promoting the fresh vitality of the new generation of artists and writers.[9]

In the end Bachelard's *Lautréamont*, while perhaps less attractive than his later, better known studies of the imagination, is nevertheless the most revealing. It demonstrates that his critical faculties were always awake; that his reading was not desultory nor his reflections on poetry merely associative in character. *Lautréamont* is a book of exemplary discipline. Its author gives his subject the full attention it deserves and enters totally into the spirit of energy, aggression, and violence that it evokes. But he does not remain trapped there. Having made as careful and generous an assessment as

9.   All cited from *Ezra Pound and the Visual Arts*, ed. Harriet Zinnes (New York, 1980), 7, 9, 302, 151, 303, 152.

possible of this extraordinary work, he looks beyond it to suggest where the next steps might lead and where he stands in relation to Lautréamontism. Bachelard's posture is dialectical; one must understand, even live out Lautréamontism if he is to go beyond it, for even *Maldoror* is not immune to becoming an inert and academic classic. The projective life of the imagination, faithfully pursued, can lead us beyond Lautréamont himself and the sterile hero-worship of the "voices of the past" to the living power of the word and the image that Bachelard was to extoll for the remaining decades of his life.

The most important aspect of Bachelard's contribution is, then, his defense of the creative impulse, for the imagination does have moral meaning, though not necessarily the openly didactic sort that the naïve moralist would demand. Bachelard seems to imply what Wallace Stevens, only three years after the publication of this book, was also saying: "The mind has added nothing to human nature. It is a violence from within that protects us from a violence without. It is the imagination pressing back against the pressure of reality. It seems, in the last analysis, to have something to do with our self-preservation; and that, no doubt, is why the expression of it, the sound of its words, helps us to live our lives."[10]

10. Wallace Stevens, "The Noble Rider and the Sound of Words," in *The Necessary Angel* (New York, 1951), 36.

Index to *Lautréamont*